UNQUALIFIED

WHERE YOU CAN BEGIN TO BE GREAT

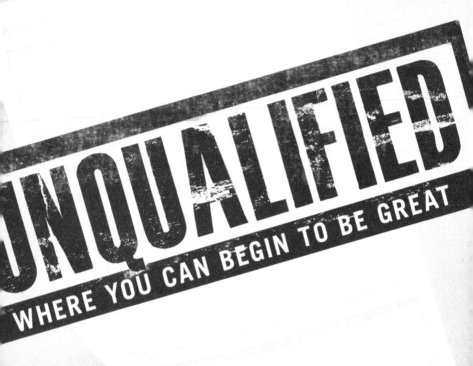

UNQUALIFIED
WHERE YOU CAN BEGIN TO BE GREAT

PAT SCHATZLINE

CHARISMA
HOUSE

Most CHARISMA HOUSE BOOK GROUP products are available at special quantity discounts for bulk purchase for sales promotions, premiums, fund-raising, and educational needs. For details, write Charisma House Book Group, 600 Rinehart Road, Lake Mary, Florida 32746, or telephone (407) 333-0600.

UNQUALIFIED by Pat Schatzline
Published by Charisma House
Charisma Media/Charisma House Book Group
600 Rinehart Road
Lake Mary, Florida 32746
www.charismahouse.com

Cover design by Justin Evans

Visit the author's website at www.theunqualified.com.

Library of Congress Cataloging-in-Publication Data:
An application to register this book for cataloging has been submitted to the Library of Congress.
International Standard Book Number: 978-1-62998-612-8
E-book ISBN: 978-1-62998-613-5

First edition

15 16 17 18 19 — 987654321
Printed in the United States of America

This book will allow you to break through your past and step into God's destiny. If you are unqualified plus Jesus, you are qualified and chosen to be front and center for the greatest harvest in history.

—SID ROTH
HOST, *IT'S SUPERNATURAL!*

Pat Schatzline is a powerful voice of ministry. His books are full of revelation that help youth and their leaders see the value that God has placed in them. This book will equip you with powerful tools and hope that God's plan for you is far from over.

—JOE CHAMPION
PASTOR, CELEBRATION CHURCH, AUSTIN, TEXAS

With his latest book Pat Schatzline fills a much-needed gap of understanding for all believers who feel called into the ministry but feel unqualified, ill-equipped, or disqualified because of their past failures, lack of education, or gifts. It's a practical book helping folks who feel like "nobodies." It shows how God makes them into "somebodies." This book will help change the course of the church for generations to come.

—MARCUS D. LAMB
FOUNDER AND PRESIDENT, DAYSTAR TELEVISION
NETWORK

It has been a very long time since I have read any book that I relate to more than this one. Pat Schatzline has penned a masterpiece. This is not a "how-to" book—it is an "I cannot do this if God does not help me" book. I love it!

—JOHN A. KILPATRICK
FOUNDER AND SENIOR PASTOR
CHURCH OF HIS PRESENCE, DAPHNE, ALABAMA

God is using Pat Schatzline to remind people that it only takes a remnant to change our world. The people God uses at times are the people who realize that God is the only one that can help us reach our full potential. This book will not only bless you but also encourage you that God takes the nothings of this world and makes them somebodies.

—STEVE SMOTHERMON SR.
PASTOR, LEGACY CHURCH, ALBUQUERQUE, NEW MEXICO

Unqualified wonderfully dismantles societal and individual strongholds that dishonor the splendor of God's grace. For too long religious culture has required ordinations, rule-keeping, or certificates from the right denominations as the means to qualify someone to participate in the activities of God in the earth. *Unqualified* removes excuses and opens a gospel-based hope into the freedom of high-level partnership with God.

Scripture announces that without a vision, the people perish. Scripture also suggests and alludes to the reality that without people, the vision perishes. Pat's timely writing will activate latent yearnings of God's called ones, casting off condemnation and damaged identity issues and mobilizing passionate hearts. Readers of *Unqualified* lose all excuses to remain spectators in the adventures of God's kingdom.

—JIM HENNESY
AUTHOR AND PASTOR, TRINITY CHURCH
CEDAR HILL, TEXAS

My friend Pat Schatzline has written a powerful book that will bring healing to every person who has ever believed they are unfit. God is raising up "the unqualified"! In Pat's new book he confronts the lies of the enemy and the traps the enemy will use to stop God's people from fulfilling their God-given destiny. Every person whom God has ever used has felt unqualified for the job. Yet, regardless of the dark times, struggles, and the battles we face, we must rise past the pain. Each one of us has an anointing that was won at the cross! God is cheering you on! This book is a must-read for today's believers! No more excuses! We are the unqualified whom God has qualified!

—RICH WILKERSON SR.
SENIOR PASTOR, TRINITY CHURCH, MIAMI, FLORIDA

Have you ever thought, "God can't use me. I'm not gifted or talented enough. He would choose somebody else who hasn't messed up." Pat's new book will debunk this lie and show you why God has already qualified you to achieve greatness for His glory!

—AL BRICE
SENIOR PASTOR, COVENANT LOVE CHURCH
FAYETTEVILLE, NORTH CAROLINA

Unqualified! What a succinct word to describe the majority of God's servants in Scripture. God loves taking the insignificant, the weak, the seemingly foolish, and the lowly—aka the unqualified—and manifesting His power and wisdom through them so that no one will doubt that it is not us but the excellence of the power that dwells within us. The more we realize how unqualified we are, the greater our effectiveness. So if you think you are unqualified, then read this. For those who think you are qualified, read this as well. You will be convinced to come join the band of unqualified brothers.

—REV. YANG TUCK YOONG
FOUNDER AND SENIOR PASTOR
CORNERSTONE COMMUNITY CHURCH, SINGAPORE

We are living in perilous times that demand a revival that renews our understanding of who God has called us to be and reshapes the culture of God's people. Pat offers his readers an opportunity to come and take their place in the kingdom of God in these final hours of time. He unveils for each person a place where they too can stand together with Christ Jesus and shine as lights in a dark age. He will inspire you to find your identity in that which the system of this world rejects but that God will magnify through exploits.

—MARK SPITSBERGEN
PASTOR, ABIDING PLACE, SAN DIEGO, CALIFORNIA

Pat has invited us to realize the power of our journey in Jesus. Through his writings he has brought to our attention our need for spiritual progress. Within each of us is an innate desire to return to the perfect world that Adam lost. In this book Pat moves us from our personal journey to the possibilities of discovering and releasing the gifting within us that aids others on their journey. It contains incredible insight into who we were created and appointed to become. Prepare to be lost in your own potential.

—BISHOP PATRICK M. SCHATZLINE, DMIN
FOUNDER, DAYSTAR MINISTRIES INTERNATIONAL

Pat's newest book, *Unqualified*, proves once again the fact that these are the kinds of folks God seems to recruit for His team! Pat feels "unqualified" to be an author, and I feel "unqualified" to write this endorsement. In fact, it seems like only the "unqualified" people reading this book will be the ones truly used by the Lord in these last days before the Lord's return. I love Pat and am thankful his "unqualified" voice is touching multitudes with the gospel of Christ!

—BISHOP DAVID. L. THOMAS
PASTOR, VICTORY CHRISTIAN CENTER
YOUNGSTOWN, OHIO

Not surprisingly Pat Schatzline has once again put his finger on the pulse of a generation longing to find purpose and fulfill destiny. This book is a rallying cry for the army of God, challenging and coercing readers to lay aside excuses, comparisons, and insecurities, and march in their identity as anointed and confident kingdom influencers.

—Jay Stewart
Lead pastor, The Refuge
Concord, North Carolina

This is not just another book, but a *revelation* for a *revolution*! Pat's last book, *I Am Remnant*, awakened a generation to their end-time identity. *Unqualified* will *activate* that generation to their end-time destiny to *serve, shake,* and *shock* the world into the kingdom of God!

—Paul Owens
Pastor, Fresh Start Church, Peoria, Arizona

Thank you, Pat, for another book that carries a message from the heart of God. What could be more of an expression of God's grace than how He uses and chooses the "unqualified"? In a culture that now calls "reality" sitting on the sidelines while watching others live, you have given everyone an invitation to get into the game. Someone has said that God does not call the qualified, He qualifies those He has called. This book will be used to call forth an army of conquerors who had thought they were overlooked and undervalued.

—George Sawyer
Author, pastor, Calvary, Decatur, Alabama

This book should come with a warning label! I found myself being described in the pages of this book, even to the words I have said within myself. I always struggled with my embarrassing family history, weak education background, and lack of "qualifications," and I wondered why He would still choose me. If you have ever wondered why God chose you, then read this!

—Chris Estrada
Director, youth major for
Christ for the Nations Institute
Founder, Chris Estrada Ministries

Pat Schatzline has captured the heart of a generation and shows how they can still be loved, accepted, and respond to the divine purpose for which they were created. This book is written for and to a generation who, like every Bible character, found their purpose in God through Christ. Being one of the "unqualified," I have found security, fulfillment, and strength in learning that Christ's grace has qualified me. This is a must-read for both young and old alike—for those who are unchurched as well as those who are well churched. This book will cause you to change the label of your life from "unqualified" to "qualified."

—Donald L. Gibson
Author, pastor, Mercy Gate Church
Mont Belvieu, Texas

In his new book Pat teaches us that God, exclusively, uses "unqualified" people to change the world because that's the only kind of people who exist. If you think you are unqualified for your calling, then this book is for you.

—Doug McAllister
Author, pastor, Journey Fellowship Church
www.journeyfellowshipchurch.com

This book will reach to the core of all that you think you know about the truth in the Word. Even as a Christian you may battle past or even your present obstacles Satan puts before you. Most of us deal with insecurities, and Satan wants to keep that at the forefront of our mind-set. Pat uncovers the truth in God's Word that God wants to reach the hurt and broken—the unqualified—by using us: the unqualified.

The truth Pat reveals in his new book will set you free to fulfill God's calling on your life no matter where you've come from, where you are now, or where you think you're headed. This is an easy read with revelation of the truth and character of God. I pray a spirit of revelation over you as you read his follow-up to *I Am Remnant*. Set your heart to take in the truths Pat will reveal to you in *Unqualified*. Thank you to this amazing man of God who has walked the walk and is now talking the talk. Pat, we honor you and this book! May many be impacted and changed for all eternity and go set the world on fire equipped with the truths you reveal!

—Tim Roberts
President, Kingdom Resources Marketplace Ministries

I often asked myself why God would pick me until I realized that in the last days (which we are living in) God is raising up the "no name" and "no-face" people out of obscurity for His *revival*! Pat's book *Unqualified* helps awaken the reality that it is really about the *He* in *me*! Even through our past pain and trials we learn to say like the psalmist, "It was good that I was afflicted for then I learned the statutes of the Lord" (Ps. 119:71). God took what was meant for evil and used it for His good. This book, which I liken to a modern-day energy drink, will surely awaken every reader to their God-given destiny and kingdom assignment. *What a book*!

—Scott S. Schatzline
Lead pastor, Daystar Family Churches
Northport, Alabama

So many feel disqualified to do anything meaningful for God, but in Pat's latest book, *Unqualified*, we see God's plan to use absolutely *anyone* who is willing. Jesus delights in moving us from obscurity into significance to make His name known. Pat really hits the nail on the head by helping us understand our rightful place and by avoiding the pitfalls the enemy creates to undermine God's plan.

—Jamie Jones
Lead pastor, Trinity Assembly of God
Deltona, Florida

Pastor Pat's book *Unqualified* is the very heartbeat of God. This book is a love song from God to an entire generation of radicals. I highly recommend this book, but be warned: it will offend you in all the right places!

—LUKE HOLTER
AWARD–WINNING AUTHOR AND PROPHETIC VOICE

Throughout God's Word we consistently observe this powerful insight into God's character: God delights in using messed-up people to manifest and shine His enabling power and grace through. For example, God must have known of Samson's propensity to be undisciplined and a womanizer, yet He chose him to deliver and rule Israel. God sovereignly called a prostitute named Rahab, not only to guarantee Israel's conquest of Jericho but to also be included in Jesus's ancestry.

Pat Schatzline has written another masterpiece in the spirit of *Why Is God So Mad at Me?* and *I Am Remnant* to help the reader overcome the weapons of inferiority and condemnation that Satan uses to distract, demoralize, and detour him into thinking he can ever be good enough to be used by God to do great and mighty things.

This book is not vague theology but a down-to-earth exposé of Satan's lies and God's overwhelming desire to use anyone human enough to have messed up in life or who is struggling with mediocrity and low self-worth. The tenets of "The Manifesto of the Unqualified" are sufficient reason to purchase this powerful book. Truly this book will challenge and commission all to confront the guilts of the past and the apprehensions with the future, and rise up to grasp today with the confidence that God wants to and will use them to do great and mighty things for His kingdom!!

—DAVID GARCIA
AUTHOR AND PASTOR OF GRACE WORLD OUTREACH
CHURCH, BROOKSVILLE, FLORIDA

Pastor Pat Schatzline has a true gift in seeing God's call for the unqualified. He saw me when I wasn't much and believed in me and spoke over me that God would use me. He was right! And today all that I thought disqualified me for ministry are the exact things God has used to qualify me. This book is a must-read for anyone who thinks he has gone too far, lived too long, sinned too much, or is too young, too dumb, or whatever it may be. Read this book and know you are qualified!

—JEREMY DONOVAN
AUTHOR, PASTOR, AND DIRECTOR OF STUDENT
MINISTRIES, TRINITY CHURCH, CEDAR HILL, TEXAS

Pat Schatzline has done it again! Reading this book has ignited a fresh fire within to make my life count. This book is a stirring war cry to a generation God is calling to awaken and take their place! This book will challenge *you* to believe that God wants to use *you* to change the world!

—MICHAEL DOW
EVANGELIST AND FOUNDER, BURNING ONES

I dedicate this book to my amazing dad and mom, Bishop Patrick and Deb Schatzline. When I was a boy, you decided Jesus must be the head of our home. I watched you sacrifice and lay everything down for the call of God. The price you paid for our family is incalculable. Our family was so unqualified, but you refused to give up. You pastored places that few would have gone to lead, and you restored lost value to the "least of these." You have handled victory and heartache with the amazing grace of God. You taught us that we could do anything for God, because in our weakness Christ is made strong. You are rescuers of the unqualified. Thank you for believing in me! I love and honor you.

I also dedicate this book to my son, Nate, my daughter, Abby, my daughter-in-law, Adrienne, and my grandson, Jack. You bring me more joy than I can say! I believe that you are truly gifts from the Lord. We must not stop leading a generation into the arms of a loving Savior. God has anointed you to be His voice. You carry on the mantle of the unqualified remnant. God will use you to go where Mom and I could not. This is your moment! I am so proud of you!

CONTENTS

Acknowledgments xviii
Foreword by Glen Berteau.......................... xx
Introduction 1

Section I
The Rise of the Unqualified

1   "Ah, Sovereign Lord!" 13
2   How Could God Use Me? 33
3   The Messiah's Misfits 45
4   You Are Not Plan B.......................... 62
5   Royalty Sometimes Comes Broken 76

Section II
The Unqualified Must Experience...

6   The Separation............................... 94
7   Rehiring the Holy Spirit..................... 117
8   Wilderness Wanderers 133

Section III
Don't Get Disqualified!

9   The Eight Insatiable Absolutes
    of the Unqualified 150
10 You Can't Cut My Hair!..................... 179
11 The Lion, the Corpse, and the Donkey 199

Section IV
The Rise of the Unqualified

12 Get Your Feet Ready........................ 210
13 You Are God's Hashtag 217
Notes 225

ACKNOWLEDGMENTS

I FIRST MUST THANK my beautiful and anointed wife, Karen. Thank you for allowing me this season to get this message out the world. You are truly my greatest encourager and voice of reason. I stand amazed at the anointing and wisdom that you walk in daily. You are my hero and the wind beneath my wings! I love you!

Thank you to my amazing in-laws, John and Gail Brown. You are voices of love, compassion, and civility in a crazy world. Your encouragement pushes me to dream big dreams. Your simplicity is what makes people desire to know you. I love you.

Thank you to Dr. Connie Lawrence for guiding me once again. You not only helped me to organize this vision but also helped to bring it to life on paper with your hard work. I couldn't have done it without you!

Thank you so much to my assistant and spiritual daughter, Jamie Kowalski, who works so hard to help Karen and me accomplish the call of God. Your countless hours and hard work are incredible. We love you!

Thank you to Debbie Marrie, Adrienne Gaines, Woodley Auguste, Ann Mulchan, SueLee Hamilton, Marcos Perez, and the entire team at Charisma Media. You are truly a joy to work with. Your relentless pursuit of the right message to bring healing to the world inspires me.

To the board and ministry supporters of Remnant Ministries International: thank you for believing in the message that God has given Karen and me. We love and honor you deeply!

Lastly, to those who are on the front lines, proclaiming the unadulterated Word of God, I say, "THANK YOU!" Do not stop what you are doing. You are making a difference. Your reward awaits your arrival at the throne. We must keep pressing toward the high call!

FOREWORD

How did God pick me as a minister? No one in my family had ever been a Christian. No relatives were missionaries, Sunday school teachers, or even church ushers. Bibles were not in my house, and God lived in a cloud somewhere.

I am unqualified. I definitely lacked the qualifications necessary to participate in any area of ministry. I was not born in a minister's home, was not connected to a church, and did not possess a degree from Bible school. I am unqualified in comparison to those blessed by spiritual fathers and mentors.

In reality I am unqualified only by my own assessment, downloaded from my fleshly thinking.

Unqualified is actually a supernatural, penetrating, prophetic word of qualification on every résumé God promotes to greatness. You can't (you're unqualified), but He can (He qualifies you).

Read who you really are and what you were born for. Discover the seed of potential God has placed inside you. Pat Schatzline bravely and masterfully confronts this secret society of the unqualified. Get ready to be transformed.

—GLEN BERTEAU
AUTHOR AND SENIOR PASTOR, THE HOUSE
MODESTO, CALIFORNIA

INTRODUCTION

Warning:

- Do not read this book if you do not want to be used by God.
- Do not read this book if you would rather have crutches than wings.
- Do not read this book if you are unwilling to lay down your excuses and pick up a mandate from heaven.
- Do not read this book if you are satisfied blaming everyone else for your mundane life.
- Do not read this book if you will not throw down your walking cane and put on your running shoes.
- Do not read this book if you do not burn deep within to be used by God to make a difference.

Why did I open this book with a warning? Because I believe this book will remove the excuses and lethargy that may plague your life and most definitely plagues this generation. I must ask: Are you ready for the adventure of a lifetime? You can step into that adventure when you realize God doesn't necessarily call the qualified but always qualifies the called.

But wait. I can hear your protests now: "How in the world could God ever use me? I'm just not qualified!"

Those are the words I've heard from people all over the

world. Sadly they're also the words I've used against myself so many times in despair, wondering why God would choose to use me for His kingdom work. "After all," I reasoned in those moments, "if people really know who I am behind the passionate and bold veil I've created, they'll never listen to a word I share."

Believe me, I get it.

Maybe you have a tainted past. Maybe you got caught up in unsavory dealings in your youth. Maybe those dealings happened just yesterday or even this morning. Maybe you let yourself get pulled into promiscuity, drugs, sabotage, or theft. Maybe you've been a liar, a drunkard, a swindler, or a cheat. You can't imagine God would ever use you! You're completely unqualified.

Or maybe you don't have talent. You look around and see people who know what they're doing and know what they're about—and that's not you. Everyone else has found their talent and call, but you haven't. You don't speak well, you don't know a trade, you haven't been to school, or if you have you didn't perform well. You don't know a lot about the Bible. You can't sing. You're not the most attractive candidate for any job, either in the mirror or on paper. You're completely unqualified for anything having to do with God's service.

Believe me, I get all of this. And you know what? It's true. You *are* unqualified.

But that's actually the good news! God wants to use you exactly where you are, exactly because you are unqualified.

It might sound backward to hear this, but I'm going to ask you to trust me on this. Go with me for a bit here—for at least the length of this book. I want to prove it to you.

Oh, and one more thing. Lest you think you're alone in feeling this way, let me hasten to say that you're not. You're in the company of a whole cloud of witnesses who have been there too—liars, cheats, stutterers, adulterers, killers, braggarts, betrayers, and cowards. The Bible tells us they're all there—and all were used by God anyway, and sometimes *especially* because they were unqualified in their own particular ways.

I'm in this boat with you too! You'll get to hear some of my stories about being unqualified as we go through the book—ways I've felt unworthy or unprepared to be used by God in different ways, leading to so much heartache and struggle with my identity and call to join God's service over the years.

But the truth is, God chooses to use you and me regardless of all that makes us unqualified. In fact, the more hung up we are on our lack of qualifications, the less likely we are to open ourselves to being used by God in extraordinary, unexpected ways. And believe me, God definitely wants to use you that way. He wants to use all of us that way, if we simply let Him and make ourselves available for it.

So here's your litmus test for whether you should take the journey into reading this book:

1. Do you wonder if God could possibly use you?

2. Do you feel uncomfortable in religious settings?

3. Do you see others who are way more gifted than you?

4. Do you believe your past disqualifies you for service in God's kingdom?

5. Do you hear the voice of the enemy screaming, "You are such a failure!"?

6. Do you long to be an agent of change in a lost and dying world?

If you answered yes to any of these questions, then you're ready to read this book. Why? Because it means you're the unqualified remnant of God that He wants to use to change this world.

Here's the deal. God doesn't choose the best in the crowd, the most organized, the most eloquent, or the most likely to succeed. No! He chooses people like you and me—people who are simply available. In fact, take a look at what one of my favorite verses in the Bible has to say about it:

> Take a good look, friends, at who you were when you got called into this life. I don't see many of "the brightest and the best" among you, not many influential, not many from high-society families. Isn't it obvious that God deliberately chose men and women that the culture overlooks and exploits and abuses, chose these "nobodies" to expose the hollow pretensions of the "somebodies"?
> —1 CORINTHIANS 1:26–28, THE MESSAGE

In reality all of us are unqualified for God's service. But with God's help, we'll finish this life with nothing left to do. God has chosen you for such a time as this! Any scars you carry are proof you made it through the battle. Your testimony is actually a declaration that God is bigger than your past. Stop declaring you're not qualified and start saying instead, "With God all things are possible" (Matt. 19:26). God really can use the nobodies to touch the anybodies for the sake of the most important somebody, named Jesus!

Take *that*, devil!

Can God use you and me? Maybe instead the question should be, "How could God *not* use you and me?" Because the fact is, God has always chosen the ones who seemed most unqualified for His service. They're the ones who cause the devil to scream, "No way!" And God screams in response, "Yahweh!"

Throughout this book we'll look at some of the specific examples in Scripture of God using the unqualified to accomplish mighty things in His name. You'll also find quotes from well-known leaders and future leaders laced throughout the book whom God is raising up as His unqualified remnant, each one sharing what it means to be unqualified in their own words. Use those quotes as motivation to stay the path and as reaffirmation that you aren't alone in walking it.

Now before we close out this introduction, let me leave you with a manifesto God spoke to my heart as I began writing this book. It represents the truth about the unqualified that God desires to use because He can trust them with His glory. Is that you? Are you unqualified? If so, join us!

The Manifesto of the Unqualified

But God has chosen the foolish things of the world to confound the wise. God has chosen the weak things of the world to confound the things which are mighty. And God has chosen the base things of the world and things which are despised. Yes, and He chose things which did not exist to bring to nothing things that do, so that no flesh should boast in His presence.
—1 CORINTHIANS 1:27–29, MEV

- The unqualified embrace the fact that their God identity is formed in the wilderness of obscurity.
- The unqualified glance back at their past not with remorse or fear but so they may warn others of the road ahead.
- The unqualified refuse to bow to compromise because they would rather have God, not man, firmly on their side.
- The unqualified understand that without the active work of the Holy Spirit in their lives, they will become an echo rather than God's voice of deliverance.

- The unqualified would rather welcome the Holy Spirit in a small gathering of the hungry than a crowded room of the satisfied.

- The unqualified stand in awe of the love of God that rescued them from a life of pain.

- The unqualified leave their pride and fear at the doorway of God's invitation to partake of His body and blood.

- The unqualified know God is not looking for the most righteous or best voice, but rather the most obedient and faithful servant.

- The unqualified are never quick to judge because they know the righteous judge has redeemed them from their past to rescue those in their future.

- The unqualified know God uses the least qualified to change history and confound the most qualified.

- The unqualified have realized their insecurities must end at the place where God carried them the most when they were at their worst.

- The unqualified are the ones most uniquely qualified to embrace a Savior who was rejected by man and crucified on a dead tree, because they too are now dead to this world.

- The unqualified never ignore the hurting because they have scars of pain too to prove they have survived to testify.

- The unqualified realize God never demands perfection but continually whispers that we must stay in pursuit of Him.

- The unqualified have established in their hearts that the anointing of God is what makes them ready to dream again.

- The unqualified walk in reverence of the knowledge that without God's help, they will never accomplish anything.

- The unqualified live their lives continually seeking the face of God for direction, because they know without Him they are on a journey that leads to nowhere.

- The unqualified never seek the stage because they know that's not where their identity rests, seeking instead the quiet solace of secret God encounters.

- The unqualified choose to stay away from the mirror of self-deprecation and instead spend their lives looking through binoculars of hope.

- The unqualified have learned that leaning on their own understanding only delays the mission God has prepared for them.

- The unqualified stay hidden in God's Word so they never walk in the wisdom of the world.

- The unqualified continually ignore the noise of the culture the enemy uses to disqualify their voice.

- The unqualified don't have to be seen or heard because they know God has already established their journey.

- The unqualified don't mind the dark season because they know God always shines the brightest in the dark.

- The unqualified know their callings were created in the cave where God began the work that would lead them out into the world.

- The unqualified never take credit for works of God because they know the words Jesus said about "greater works shall you do" referred to those they are called to serve.

- The unqualified realized long ago that gifting and talents fail, but brokenness is the stage of transformation.

- The unqualified recognize the flaws in their armor so as not to embarrass the cross when God elevates them.

- The unqualified are quick to run from compromise because they don't want to be disqualified from the work of the King.

- The unqualified never desire the stage but know it is on the stage that they become a prop for God's glory and not their own.

- The unqualified never desire to hear the cheer from the crowd but only the cries of the great cloud of witnesses.

- The unqualified have nothing to lose because they lost all selfish ambition at the foot of the cross of humiliation.

- The unqualified have realized that if God is not able to do a work in them, then those they are called to serve will never experience the healing that comes from their Savior's redeeming love.

- The unqualified must share the truth of God because they know the enemy's lies are what previously kept them locked in a prison of pain.

- The unqualified can hear the sounds of the drowning because they know what it is like to be a drowning victim who was rescued by a Savior.

- The unqualified have learned to ignore the voice of the enemy because they know they are God's messengers of freedom.

- The unqualified quickly recognize their errors because they've seen what has disqualified other messengers of hope.

- The unqualified are desperate for a move of God in this generation so others will realize it's God's love that qualifies us for eternity.

- The unqualified never throw stones at others' failures because they are too busy throwing a rope to rescue them.

- The unqualified are never impressed with religion because they know religion is what kept them in bondage for years and crucified their Savior.

- The unqualified are those God has always used to confound man's humanistic message and law of natural selection because they represent the enemy's failed attempt to bury the living.

- The unqualified know they were never called to look like the world but instead to bring God's message of hope to the hurting.

- The unqualified are keenly aware that if God does not intervene, then they are doomed to self-destruct.

- The unqualified know that heaven will not be a country club of the elite but a fellowship of the unashamed.

- The unqualified are keenly aware that spiritual depth and desperation for God will shut the mouth of the naysayers and depose the accusations of the presumptuous.

As Smith Wigglesworth once said, "God is on His throne and can take you a thousand miles a minute in a moment. Have faith to jump into His supernatural plan."[1] God is awakening you to His plan and vision for your life. No more excuses! Buckle up. This is your moment. You are God's hashtag. You are His exclamation point at the end of His Word. It's time for God encounters. The journey starts on the next page!

"I'm the real definition of what it means to be unqualified. I've lived most of my life in an extremely disobedient fashion. I've had years of inappropriate thoughts and behavior. But when the Lord came and worked in my life, I stood up for Him and spoke out to the masses about who He was and what He did."

—Maurice Clarett, former NFL player
and entrepreneur, Columbus, OH

SECTION I
THE RISE OF THE UNQUALIFIED

Chapter 1

"AH, SOVEREIGN LORD!"

"I have never started anything that I was qualified for, but the more unqualified, the better! Even Jesus in the garden felt unqualified!"

—Philip Cameron, missionary evangelist and founder of Stella's House orphanages, Montgomery, AL

N ow is the time for the unqualified to rise and lead. Why? Because what we have been doing has not worked. The unqualified are the ones who understand they cannot accomplish anything without the help of God. Furthermore, throughout history God has never tapped the professional religious to lead a Holy Spirit awakening. It's always been the ones first ignored by culture, systems, and the religious order of the day who were nominated for those jobs. Whether it was a fugitive who led the people of Israel to the Promised Land, a harlot who rescued the spies, a young shepherd who killed a giant, or a young virgin who was visited by an angel, God has chosen the ones not on the radar to accomplish His next work.

I believe God does this to show that the wisdom of man can never override the insight of God. What man calls forgotten, God calls forged. God is a scene interrupter! He loves to interrupt the scene so everyone has to sit back and say, "Only God!"

This Is Who God Is

As I began writing this chapter, I received a text on my phone from someone very dear to my wife, Karen, and me. The text was sent from pastor Phyllis Sawyer from Calvary Assembly in Decatur, Alabama. Karen and I had worked for Pastors George and Phyllis as youth pastors prior to launching as evangelists in 1997. They have always been a rock that we have turned to for direction and wisdom.

Phyllis was in a time of prayer and fasting when she wrote the text. As I studied her words, my eyes were filled with tears. The message was simple but profound. Here is what she wrote:

> He is…
>
> Our God is never changing—"He is unique, and who can make Him change? And whatever His soul desires, that He does." Job 23:13
>
> Our God is the first and last—"Thus saith the Lord, the King of Israel, and his Redeemer, the Lord of hosts; 'I am the First and I am the Last; besides Me there is no God." Isaiah 44:6 [kjv]
>
> Our God is King forever and ever—"The Lord is King forever and ever; the nations have perished out of His land." Psalm 10:16
>
> Our God is the beginning and the end—"I am the Alpha and the Omega, the Beginning and the End, the First and the Last." Revelation 22:13
>
> Our God is THE WORD—"He was clothed with a robe dipped in blood, and His name is called The Word of God." Revelation 19:13
>
> Today, my friend, He is our All! He is EVERYTHING we want and need! He is! He is! He is!
>
> My God is the one who steps on mountains and makes them crumble! [Habbakuk 3:6.]
>
> "I am the Lord, the God of all flesh. Is there anything too hard for Me?" [Jeremiah 32:27.]
>
> My prayer for you today is that you discover a

revelation that is just your revelation of who and what
God is in you and for you.

This text really says it all—*our God is!* The text declares
God is sovereign. When we begin to understand the sovereignty of God, we become candidates for the miraculous.
When God calls you into His kingdom work, the greatest
hindrance you will face is not whether someone opens
doors for you or gives you a hand up the ladder of ministry.
No, the greatest hindrance to your call is the belief that you
can make it happen yourself.

We must understand that our nation is deeply in need of
a reformation. We are now living in a time when truth is
considered hate speech, and very soon in many places the
only intolerance that will be acceptable is bigotry toward
those who declare God's Word and refuse to condone
ungodly lifestyles.

The atmosphere we now live in is enough to make God's
leaders discouraged and weary. But we must not grow weary
in well doing, for it is at a time like this that we must trust
the Lord. I believe with everything in me that if the lordship
of God is not declared and acted upon in America, then our
nation is doomed!

The Wave Dream

On Sunday morning, June 1, 2014, at about 2:00 a.m., I had a
dream I must share with you. In the dream Karen and I were
running across a map of the United States. The reason we
were running was because a giant tidal wave was chasing us.

In the dream I was screaming to Karen that we must get
people to safety. I was frantic because I knew destruction
was chasing us. As we jumped from state to state, the wave
got closer. I could hear it. I could see it. It was massive and
seemed to wipe out everything in its path. People, businesses,
and land were being swallowed up by the massive wave.

In the dream I did not fear for our lives as much as I feared our nation being destroyed. Then, suddenly, we were running up the steps of the Capitol Building in Washington, DC. As we clung to the giant white columns of the building, the wave hit, and I woke up.

I was so grieved that I began to weep before the Lord. I said, "Lord, was that destruction coming to our nation? How could this be?"

After a period of time, I fell back to sleep. When the alarm woke me a few hours later, I could not get the dream out of my mind.

That morning I ministered at a church in Tennessee. I was still grieved by the dream even after I arrived back at my hotel room that afternoon. I began to pray, saying, "Lord, You promised that You would not destroy the earth with water again. How could I have dreamed such a dream?"

Then I heard God say, "Son, the dream you had was not the destruction of America but a wave of My glory that will flood America!"

I said, "Lord, I want to see America shaken by Your glory, but it seems so far away."

The Lord then spoke again to me. He said, "Get ready, because it is coming!"

What I didn't know at the time is that Karen also had the exact same dream a few months before I did. She had even logged it in her journal the morning after she had it. Through this synchronicity of our dreams, God was speaking to us both that a wave of His glory is coming. God is calling His church back to passion, intimacy, and holiness. Don't you want to be a part of that?

For the next month I meditated on this dream time and time again. Then on the morning of July 1, 2014, I was awakened yet again with a powerful message from the Lord. I kept hearing over and over the words, "Ah, sovereign Lord!"

I didn't understand why the Lord kept speaking these

words to me. I also felt a very heavy weight in my spirit. I knew that two days later my family and I would be headed to Washington, DC, to minister with very dear friends, Drs. Rodney and Adonica Howard-Browne, at the Celebrate America Conference. The Howard-Brownes carry a very powerful prophetic mantle to awaken America to revival. The conference was going to be held at Constitution Hall and would last a total of three weeks, during which time thousands would be saved and filled with the Holy Spirit. I had been invited to speak the night of July 3, which had been deemed youth night.

As I reflected on the upcoming speaking engagement in our nation's capital and kept hearing those words, "Ah, sovereign Lord!" I became overwhelmed by the fact that God's sovereignty is what our nation is missing.

> "I have always known that because God so miraculously rescued me that He would also use me. God always uses the unqualified to fulfill His commission. This ensures that no man can take credit. God likes those of us that are pulled from the depths of sin and anoints us to do the same for others. We are those who have the testimony that begins with 'If it had not been for Jesus!'"
>
> —Jay Haizlip, pastor, author, professional skateboarder, and reality television personality on *Preachers of LA*

I began to study this phrase, "Ah, sovereign Lord!" and discovered it appears throughout the Bible. In fact, the phrase *sovereign Lord* is found 288 times in the New International Version of the Bible. One of the scriptures that stood out the most to me concerning this is found in the book of the weeping prophet Jeremiah, who said, "Ah, Sovereign LORD, you have made the heavens and the earth by your great power and outstretched arm. Nothing is too hard for you" (Jer. 32:17).

I knew that I had to go deeper in my research.

The "Ah" in My Spirit

I first began to study the word *ah* and realized it means, "an exclamation of sorrow or regret,"[1] and can be found in passages such as Psalm 35:25; Isaiah 1:24; Jeremiah 1:6; 4:10; and Jonah 4:2. I knew immediately then that the heaviness in my spirit was a cry of sorrow.

Perhaps you have noticed that many times in the Scriptures you find the word *O* just before you see *God* or *Lord*. This is the same exclamation. It is the sound you or I make when we feel deep pain. It is a cry from within—a deep yearning in the spirit. The best way I can explain it is to say it's what we're feeling when we have a breakthrough or experience great grief. It's placed as a prefix before God's name to render that same indication of emotion in the Scriptures.

I then began to study the term *sovereign Lord*. I first looked up the words in the original Hebrew language. The term for *sovereign Lord* used in the Hebrew language is *Adonai Yahweh*.[2] So let's break down those two words.

1. The meaning of *Adonai*, also meaning *Elohim*, means "all authority and exalted position." The word stresses man's relationship to God as his master, authority, and provider.[3] Moses declared of God, "Sovereign LORD, you have begun to show to your servant your greatness and your strong hand. For what god is there in heaven or on earth who can do the deeds and mighty works you do?" (Deut. 3:24).

2. The meaning of *Yahweh*[4] is "the LORD" (all caps!) from the meaning "I AM,"[5] taken from Exodus 3:14, where God said to Moses, "I AM

WHO I AM. This is what you are to say to the
Israelites: 'I AM has sent me to you.'"

"Ah, sovereign Lord" means, then, "In my anguish I declare
that all authority belongs to the I AM!" This is exactly what
happens when we give our hearts to God completely. After
all, lordship is where it begins for us! As Romans 10:9 says,
"If you declare with your mouth, 'Jesus is Lord,' and believe
in your heart that God raised Him from the dead, you will
be saved."

Tracking the Source of the Burden

At first I wondered why this phrase was so heavy on my spirit.
I wondered if it could be because the Supreme Court of the
United States had just ruled four days prior on the side of
Hobby Lobby, in a 5–4 decision, that Hobby Lobby did not
have to provide contraception that could kill a child in the
womb on the basis of religious convictions.[6] After all, Psalm
109:21 says, "But you, Sovereign LORD, help me for your
name's sake; out of the goodness of your love, deliver me."

Maybe it was because I have desired so badly for the
youth of this generation to have an early encounter with
God and make Him all that matters, as it says in Psalm 71:5:
"For you have been my hope, Sovereign LORD, my confidence
since my youth."

Maybe it was because Islamic terrorists were beheading
journalists and issuing an Islamic jihad to America and the
Middle East. After all, the cry of Psalm 140:7 is, "Sovereign
LORD, my strong deliverer, you shield my head in the day of
battle."

I know too that God has promised to pour out His Spirit
across the land, so maybe that was it. Maybe my soul was
longing for this. After all, Isaiah 61:11 says, "For as the soil
makes the sprout come up and a garden causes seeds to

grow, so the Sovereign LORD will make righteousness and praise spring up before all nations."

Or maybe it had to do with the way secular humanism has made its way from the universities into the lives of naïve Christians. Humanism cannot harm God's plan for the church unless the church no longer sees humanism as dangerous and embraces its lies as truth. We have gone from Scripture promise boxes that you can get from Christian bookstores to Christian celebrity tweets. Many times the messages from such Christian celebrities contain more humanism than God's Word. But God has called us to declare Him and not our secular ideas and opinions: "But as for me, it is good to be near God. I have made the Sovereign LORD my refuge; I will tell of all your deeds" (Ps. 73:28).

Maybe too it was because I was in the midst of a long summer of ministry and I live the promise of Isaiah 61:1: "The Spirit of the Sovereign LORD is on me, because the LORD has anointed me to proclaim good news to the poor. He has sent me to bind up the brokenhearted, to proclaim freedom for the captives and release from darkness for the prisoners." How can I help but be burdened in my spirit when carrying such purpose in my heart?

Or maybe it's because I was—and continue to be—so grieved by the false grace movement spreading across America that has removed repentance from salvation. Jude 1:4 says it like this: "For certain individuals whose condemnation was written about long ago have secretly slipped in among you. They are ungodly people, who pervert the grace of our God into a license for immorality and deny Jesus Christ our only Sovereign and Lord."

One of my heroes is Dietrich Bonhoeffer, the German Lutheran pastor who stood against Hitler and the Nazis during World War II. This great theologian watched as the government infiltrated the church, insisting that it preach Nazi propaganda. Dietrich Bonhoeffer refused to bow. He and many others from the group called the Confessing Church stood their ground. He would later be murdered by Hitler and his regime. Yet his writings still speak to us today. This theologian understood that holiness is what brings about true relationship with God. He once wrote, "Cheap grace is the grace we bestow on ourselves. Cheap grace is the preaching of forgiveness without requiring repentance, baptism without church discipline, Communion without confession....Cheap grace is grace without discipleship, grace without the cross, grace without Jesus Christ, living and incarnate."[7]

Too many Christians are unwilling to take bold stands today, perhaps because too many teachers of the gospel have bought into the lie that a lifestyle of perversion is OK with God. However, 2 Peter 2:1 warns, "But there were also false prophets among the people, just as there will be false teachers among you, who will secretly bring in destructive heresies, even denying the Lord who bought them, bringing swift destruction upon themselves" (MEV).

As I began to go deeper into my research of the phrase, though, I realized it was actually a cry from the heart of God for our nation and the army God desires to raise up. God wants to be sovereign once again in our lives and in America. When God has all authority over a nation, then His protection can cover it.

In order for this to happen, though, we must invite God back into our nation. The Bible says, "Blessed is the nation whose God is the LORD, the people whom He has chosen as His inheritance" (Ps. 33:12, MEV). This verse declares where the blessing comes from. It doesn't come from innovative minds, from the financial markets, or from the White House. The blessing of God comes when we declare that Jesus is Lord of our nation.

We Need God's Help

You must realize that without God's intervention, our nation is doomed to self-destruct. This may sound very unpatriotic, but my patriotism is at the root of why I would make such a statement. I believe God is not done with America—and He wants to use us, the unqualified, to accomplish His purposes.

I believe Satan's ultimate goal is to destroy this nation. America has sent Christian missionaries all over the world to spread the gospel for more than two hundred years. Alas, it might be time for the missionaries to come home, because our nation needs their pioneer spirits and their unabashed voices.

In fact, the church at large is very quiet concerning the moral issues of today. Maybe this is due to a fear of offending the lost or causing a flap in the media. In any case, if Satan can quiet the church concerning righteous and moral issues, he will have freedom to roam at will, unabated by "those pesky Christians."

"The filth, the vile, the unrighteousness, and thoughts I fight daily to walk on the right path carrying the love of Christ make the word *unqualified* my middle name. I am amazed that a perfect God would give a putrid person with such a terrible past the gift of salvation! I cry mercy and grace on all occasions. Now I can show the lost His love with my gifts!"

—Steve McGranahan, strongman and TV personality on *Fat N' Furious*

This is why I'm convinced that if the unqualified and the remnant do not rise up and lead, then we as a church will be done in by our plastic faith and lost holiness. While we have spent the last fifty years building our majestic houses of worship, the nation has lost its magnificent voice of truth.

To see the devil's handiwork, all you have to do is tune into the twenty-four-hour cable news cycle or pick up a newspaper. I believe we are now living in a day when the books of prophecy, such as Daniel, Isaiah, Ezekiel, Amos, 1 and 2 Thessalonians, and Revelation, are being unfolded and fulfilled in front of our very eyes. Whether we look at the continued advance of Islamic militants, the isolation and persecution of Israel, the constant threat of horrible diseases, the economic uncertainty that plagues us (the US national debt raced past eighteen trillion dollars as of the writing of this book[8]), or the rise of the anti-Christian agenda, we know we are in very perilous times.

The destruction of America will come from those inside it, not outside. Those who have decided that God is no longer welcome on our soil have eroded the very foundation of Christianity. Biblical values are now considered closed-minded and obsolete by the humanist, atheist, and progressive culture. The systematic dismantling of our nation's history came to a head when the forty-fourth president of the United States, Barack Obama, declared at a press conference in the nation of Turkey on April 6, 2009, "We do not consider ourselves a Christian nation."[9] This, of course, was our president doing his best to win the hearts of the Middle East in what many have called his "apology tour."[10] It has not necessarily worked out very well for our president or our nation, since the majority of the Muslim world hates America now more than ever.[11] Yet this also exposes an agenda that is at work in our nation. The agenda includes the intense demonization of those who stand for biblical truth in areas such as heterosexual marriage, gender identification, the protection of the unborn, and similar moral issues.

The Forgotten Lordship

For centuries the world needed to only look to the West, to a young, idealistic nation called America, for direction and strength. From the days at Plymouth Rock to the wars of the Middle East, we have stood as a beacon of hope.

What has made our nation so special is the foundation it was built upon that freedom is a right. The writers of the Declaration of Independence wrote, "We hold these truths to be self-evident, that all men are created equal, that they are endowed by their Creator with certain unalienable Rights, that among these are Life, Liberty and the pursuit of Happiness."[12] Even at the foundation of our nation, the Creator was acknowledged.

We must admit that America has not been perfect. Our history concerning the rights of all people regardless of color or creed, the equality of women, the respect of Native Americans, and the protection of the unborn has stained the landscape of our nation, but America has, for the most part, been a beacon of hope. It is a nation that has stood as the model of democracy and liberty to all abroad. Our shores represented hope, prosperity, and freedom to the world.

For more than two hundred years the fortitude and perseverance of the American culture could be tied to its founding as a Christian nation. After all, our national motto is "In God We Trust," and it was our first president, George Washington, who declared in his Thanksgiving proclamation on October 3, 1789, "It is the duty of all nations to acknowledge the providence of Almighty God, to obey His will, to be grateful for His benefits, and humbly to implore His protection and favor."[13]

All through our history as a nation, God has been confirmed as America's foundation. Here are some very important quotes that prove the sovereignty of God in our nation's history:

We have this day [Fourth of July] restored the Sovereign to whom all men ought to be obedient. He reigns in Heaven, and from the rising to the setting of the sun, let His Kingdom come.

—Samuel Adams[14]

The name of the Lord (says the Scripture) is a strong tower; thither the righteous flee and are safe (Proverbs 18:10). Let us secure His favor and He will lead us through the journey of this life and at length receive us to a better.

—Samuel Adams[15]

Our Constitution was made only for a moral and religious people. It is wholly inadequate to the government of any other.

—John Adams[16]

Providence has given to our people the choice of their rulers, and it is their duty—as well as privilege and interest—of our Christian nation to select and prefer Christians for their rulers.

—John Jay
first chief justice of the Supreme Court[17]

God who gave us life gave us liberty. Can the liberties of a nation be secure when we have removed a conviction that these liberties are the gift of God? Indeed I tremble for my country when I reflect that God is just, that His justice cannot sleep forever. —Thomas Jefferson[18]

That this nation, under God, shall have a new birth of freedom—and that government of the people, by the people, for the people, shall not perish from the earth.

—Abraham Lincoln[19]

If any earthly institution or custom conflicts with God's will, it is your Christian duty to oppose it. You must never allow the transitory, evanescent demands of man-made institutions to take precedence over the eternal demands of the Almighty God.

—MARTIN LUTHER KING JR.[20]

The Bible and its teachings helped form the basis for the Founding Fathers' abiding belief in the inalienable rights of the individual, rights which they found implicit in the Bible's teachings of the inherent worth and dignity of each individual. This same sense of man patterned the convictions of those who framed the English system of law inherited by our own Nation, as well as the ideals set forth in the Declaration of Independence and the Constitution.

—RONALD REAGAN[21]

Many secularists would love our history revised to remove God from our nation's foundation, but as you can see, the proof of God's sovereignty can be found throughout our history books and is inscribed upon the walls and monuments of our nation.

To give you an example of their intent, though, note these happenings. In 2013 a group of atheists sued the Treasury Department of the United States to try and have the words "In God We Trust" removed from US currency. These words were first approved for use on US coins during the Civil War in 1864. In 1956 Congress "passed a resolution to recognize the words officially as the national motto, replacing the de facto phrase 'E Pluribus Unum.' A year later, it began being printed on paper money."[22]

The atheists lost their battle when the US district judge dismissed the case. Judge Harold Baer Jr., in his dismissal, wrote that "the Supreme Court has repeatedly assumed the motto's secular purpose and effect," saying the federal appeals courts "have found no constitutional violation in the motto's inclusion on currency" and that the phrase's inclusion on US currency doesn't constitute a "substantial burden" on atheists.[23]

The battle to remove God from our nation will always exist. In 2014 the American Humanist Association launched a campaign called "Boycott the Pledge" on its website because the Pledge of Allegiance has the words *under God* in it.[24] These are just a few examples of efforts that are taking place on a mass scale today to remove the Christian heritage and foundation of our nation.

This is why we need the unqualified to rise up and lead more than ever before.

We Are God's Army

It's so easy for us to believe God will use someone else when He wants to use us. For years I thought if I simply knew the right people and if I developed the right gifts, then I could be qualified for service in God's massive kingdom. As we journey into the understanding that God is in the business of using the unqualified to do His work, we must also realize the unqualified will spend their entire lives doing battle with the idea that God can only use those who are qualified by culture or those who are part of the religious establishment or those who have climbed the ladder of success. Really the only high place God has called us to climb is a cross.

> I have been crucified with Christ and I no longer live, but Christ lives in me. The life I now live in the body, I live by faith in the Son of God, who loved me and gave himself for me.
> —GALATIANS 2:20

It is from the view of the cross that you hear the cries of lost humanity. And it is only when you hear the sound of the hurting and crawl from your closet of repentance that God allows you to see the bigger picture. What is the bigger picture? It has to be one that says, "If I don't do something for God, then I have no right to complain when destruction comes."

All throughout history God has used the ones no one saw coming to awaken the masses. Whether it was a kid born in a log cabin named Abraham Lincoln, a woman sitting on a bus named Rosa Parks, or a young preacher raised on a farm named Billy Graham, our nation is rich in its history with the advancement of those no one saw coming.

Could it be that you and I are the ones God saved for this moment in history to fill the void left by the former unqualified? All God needs is people willing to stand when others bow.

> "The unqualified choose to take up their cross daily without question. They ask Father God to tie them tight to the altar so that when the pain of change comes, they can't even so much as flinch. They are one with the One who gently slays them and believe in His ability to raise them into the life He has destined them to walk in."
>
> —Cameron Brice, missionary, Fayetteville, NC

In my book *I Am Remnant* I wrote the following: "This is your moment to rise up and make your mark. Destiny is at your door, and it wants to know what history will say about you. Please realize your freedom requires a response. Are you up for the challenge to prove God right and the devil wrong?"[25] I declare the same statement once again. Will you choose to lead a life that leaves no footprint on this land you have inherited by God's awesome grace? God forbid. We are accountable to the minutes, hours, and days we live on this earth. Your life doesn't belong to you. This is your call to wake up!

Oswald Chambers said it best:

There is no such thing as a private life, or a place to hide in this world, for a man or woman who is intimately aware of and shares in the sufferings of Jesus Christ. God divides the private life of His saints and makes it a highway for the world on one hand and for Himself on the other. No human being can stand that unless he is identified with Jesus Christ. We are not sanctified for ourselves. We are called into intimacy with the gospel, and things happen that appear to have nothing to do with us. But God is getting us into fellowship with Himself. Let Him have His way. If you refuse, you will be of no value to God in His redemptive work in the world, but will be a hindrance and a stumbling block.[26]

God has marked your days on His calendar. Heaven is watching from the grandstands to see what you will do with your time on earth. You are living out your appointed time: "From one man he made all the nations, that they should inhabit the whole earth; and he marked out their appointed times in history and the boundaries of their lands" (Acts 17:26).

Are You Desperate for God's Rescue?

As I stumbled through that morning on July 1, the weight of the message of "Ah, sovereign Lord!" became overwhelming. Finally I heard the Lord speak to me. He said, "Son, the 'Ah, sovereign Lord!' that you hear in your spirit is the cry of those who have come to a place of knowing I am King and ruler, those who are broken and desperate for their God. These are those that know that without My help, My intervention, and My preeminence, everything they try will be for naught. If you will declare My sovereignty, I will intervene. My army will arise. The I AM will rescue!"

God then took me to the Book of Ezekiel, and I immediately knew what God was trying to tell me. He was calling for His army to wake up. The dream I had experienced one month earlier of the tidal wave of God's glory rising on this nation was tied to this new cry in my spirit. Here is what I read (and notice the inclusion of the *sovereign Lord* phrase multiple times!):

> The LORD took hold of me, and I was carried away by the Spirit of the LORD to a valley filled with bones. He led me all around among the bones that covered the valley floor. They were scattered everywhere across the ground and were completely dried out. Then he asked me, "Son of man, can these bones become living people again?"
>
> "O Sovereign LORD," I replied, "you alone know the answer to that."
>
> Then he said to me, "Speak a prophetic message to these bones and say, 'Dry bones, listen to the word of the LORD! This is what the Sovereign LORD says: Look! I am going to put breath into you and make you live again! I will put flesh and muscles on you and cover you with skin. I will put breath into you, and you will come to life. Then you will know that I am the LORD.'"
>
> So I spoke this message, just as he told me. Suddenly as I spoke, there was a rattling noise all across the valley. The bones of each body came together and attached themselves as complete skeletons. Then as I watched, muscles and flesh formed over bones. Then skin formed to cover their bodies, but they still had no breath in them.
>
> Then he said to me, "Speak a prophetic message to the winds, son of man. Speak a prophetic message and say, 'This is what the Sovereign LORD says: Come, O breath, from the four winds! Breathe into these dead bodies so they may live again.'"
>
> So I spoke the message as he commanded me, and breath came into their bodies. They all came to life and stood up on their feet—a great army.
>
> Then he said to me, "Son of man, these bones represent the people of Israel. They are saying, 'We have

become dry, old bones—all hope is gone. Our nation
is finished.' Therefore, prophesy to them and say, 'This
is what the Sovereign LORD says: O my people, I will
open your graves of exile and cause you to rise again.
Then I will bring you back to the land of Israel. When
this happens, O my people, you will know that I am
the LORD. I will put my Spirit in you, and you will live
again and return home to your own land. Then you
will know that I, the LORD, have spoken, and I have
done what I said. Yes, the LORD has spoken!'"
—EZEKIEL 37:1–14, NLT

This scripture declares that the nation of Israel will
awaken, but I also believe this passage is for you and me.
God will awaken those who are dead on the battlefield of
life—the ones who are no longer qualified. The bones represent those who have died with no hope. Indeed, we are
in need of the wind of God to call our bones back together.
With the Spirit of God in us, we can rise up and lead.

And so on the night of July 3, just two days after receiving
that "Ah, sovereign Lord!" message from God, I shared the
stage with a dear friend named Joel Stockstill at the Celebrate
America Conference. We were both supposed to share for
thirty minutes, but as we headed into the service, Joel said to
me, "I really feel I should only share for a few moments and
you share the word God has given you in its entirety." I was
honored he would give part of his time to me, and I knew
God was stirring the atmosphere for His message.

That night God invaded the building that sits just four
hundred yards from the White House. I didn't stand up
to preach as a politician or some renowned statesman, but
rather as a kid from Oneonta, Alabama, who had a word
from the Lord. I was overwhelmed God would use me on
such an auspicious occasion. In truth, I felt like running and
hiding just before I took to the stage to deliver this message
that was only a few days old—a message I knew was not just
for youth but also for our nation as a whole—but I stood

and let the wind of God's Spirit move through me and those gathered there. He began awakening dry bones!

Right now as you're reading this, I pray that you too will stand to your feet and declare with me, "Ah, sovereign Lord!" It is when we declare the very sovereignty of God that we are fulfilling the first of the Ten Commandments found in Exodus 20:3: "You shall have no other gods before me." There is a reason that this commandment is number one. God must be first in everything we do. When God's sovereignty takes control of our lives, we are no longer moved by opinions, personalities, or catchy doctrine but simply by the will of God.

> "The unqualified are those who have paid the price to walk closely with Jesus but have not been noticed by man for extreme gifting or personality. The playing field is being leveled by the Lord of the harvest, and the laborers of true passion are being released!"
>
> —Joel Stockstill, evangelist and prophetic voice, Dallas, TX

God is awakening His people for this last-day move of God. The vision of Ezekiel tells us that all it takes is God's Spirit.

I can hear the wind blowing, the bones rattling, and the army forming. Can you? It is the awakening of the nobodies! It is the unqualified. God has given us His promise that we will see the last-day outpouring. I believe we will see the tidal wave of God's outpouring of glory when the church declares God's sovereignty once again.

Chapter 2

HOW COULD GOD USE ME?

> "The fishermen that Jesus called were the perfect example of the unqualified, but the only qualification Jesus asked for was faith."
>
> —Randy Howell, pro bass fisherman and winner of the 2014 Bassmaster Classic, Springville, AL

WE'RE LIVING IN a day of what I call the "get by" mentality. What does that mean? It means we are all just trying to get by! We're not really living because we've made up our minds that surviving is enough. We have become much like Gideon's army in Judges 8:4, where it says they were fainting yet pursuing. The constant demands of the day can be exhausting, and so often we show up for church but are nowhere near ready to engage a powerful and awesome God. Our minds are on the coming tasks of the week—our appointments, schedules, and deadlines—not on God. I have often said that God does not demand perfection but pursuit! If the devil cannot make you sin, then he will just make you too busy to have a true relationship with God.

This mentality has caused the ones chosen by God to be used in His kingdom to simply ignore His voice or take an easy path. This will not do in today's world, where taking the easy path will never lead to the change that needs to happen. In a time when truth is viewed as the new hate speech and culture is attempting to rewrite God's Word, we need something far beyond the easy path to turn the tide. Lethargy creates an indention on the pew but will never cause a blow to the devil's demonic kingdom.

It's true, though, that it's much easier to just get by than to decide to rise up and lead. Our busyness with the mundane has caused the body of Christ to be happy with a "contain and sustain" mentality. Couple that with the fact that most Christians believe there's no way God could use them to do His great work and you have an anemic church.

I'm reminded here of Jesus's résumé and a request He made of His disciples in Matthew 9. In the midst of traveling around the countryside, getting out the word about God's love and mercy, He looked at the crowds and had such love for them that He was moved to ask His disciples to pray for a very specific thing. He asked them to petition God to open an employment agency for the called.

> Jesus went throughout all the cities and villages, teaching in their synagogues, preaching the gospel of the kingdom, and healing every sickness and every disease among the people. But when He saw the crowds, He was moved with compassion for them, because they fainted and were scattered, like sheep without a shepherd. Then He said to His disciples, "The harvest truly is plentiful, but the laborers are few. Therefore, pray to the Lord of the harvest, that He will send out laborers into His harvest."
>
> —MATTHEW 9:35–38, MEV

Jesus did several things here:

1. He got up and went.

2. He brought a message of hope.

3. He saw the needs of the people.

4. He knew people had to get busy doing the work of the kingdom.

Jesus didn't say pray for the lost or for large crowds to come. No! He prayed for workers to join the cause.

What really intrigues me about Jesus's leadership that can encourage us is that in the eyes of the religious, He was completely unqualified. He didn't come from the best, most prestigious family or hang out with the well connected in society. He simply had a mandate from His heavenly Father. That is why He would say things such as, "The words that I speak to you aren't mere words. I don't just make them up on my own. The Father who resides in me crafts each word into a divine act" (John 14:10, THE MESSAGE). Jesus knew who He was because He knew *whose* He was!

Imagine what it must have been like to hear Jesus say, "The harvest is plentiful but the workers are few. Ask the Lord of the harvest, therefore, to send out workers into His harvest field." It was as if He was crying out, "Somebody join My team—together we can change the world!"

That cry is still going out.

I'm reminded of a conference call I organized for a dear friend with several key leaders on May 15, 2014. This friend was preparing to hold the previously mentioned three-week crusade in Washington, DC, that summer. The call was very powerful, as each leader voiced his or her deep concern for where America was headed as nation. As the call progressed, the cries of the leaders on the phone for revival in America seemed to usher in a wave of God's presence over the phone. When we ended the call, I began to receive text messages from many of the leaders on the call who shared how they were weeping and rejoicing at what we all believe is the coming awakening for America.

I was very emotional too, and I began to pray as I sat in my car in a parking lot after the phone call. My heart was racing as I wondered if this could be the last Great Awakening, as promised in Joel 2:28. Yet doubt still overran my emotions. At one point I prayed, "God, how can You use all of us to make a difference in a very dark time?"

I didn't hear an answer until the next morning. Then, while in prayer, I heard God speak these words to me:

> Pat, I will use the unqualified to awaken the qualified out of their drunken stupor that has been caused by the intoxication of self-built kingdoms. These man-made kingdoms have been built upon the sand of shifting truth and a forfeited authority. The unqualified will be the ones that confound the very concept of what we have called the qualified for many generations. It's the oops, the accidents, and the nobodies that will rise up and take the place of those who have grown comfortable with the idea of maintenance faith versus miraculous faith. Let Me be very clear: You are not plan B. You are the valued of the Lord!

I was shaken to my core as God spoke those words to me. You and I are not plan B. All through history God has almost always chosen the most unqualified leaders to lead His kingdom. Why? Because God doesn't listen to polls or popular opinions when choosing His leaders. Instead, He searches out those whom He can trust with His message of hope.

> "It is the unqualified that must lead a last days revolution of truth that will, once and for all, invade darkness with a flood of His marvelous light."
> —Jordan Mason, 22, ministry student, Princeton, IN

My First Brush With Being Unqualified

As I mentioned in the introduction, yes, I really do know what it means to be unqualified for a position in God's kingdom.

I think back to the first time I felt the overwhelming sense of discouragement and despair I felt many times throughout years of ministry. The year was 1988, and I was a high school senior in Oneonta, Alabama. I had just recently taken a part-time job as a youth pastor in Birmingham. Why I was ever hired to shepherd youth while still a youth myself will always be a mystery to me! Nevertheless, a pastor saw something in me that I did not. He had asked me to take over a small youth ministry that needed someone to train students in the things of God. I laugh about it now because I was no more ready to be a youth pastor than I was to be the president of the United States. In fact, I was a youth pastor for only about ten months at that church before I left for college that fall, but I made enough mistakes to fill a book that could be titled *How Not to Youth Pastor.*

After a couple of months serving as youth pastor, I was sent to a youth pastors' conference. It was a statewide event where leaders from all over would come for a couple of days to be trained. I saw youth pastors I had seen at large youth events at this conference. Many of them were well known and had done youth ministry for many years. As a young man who wasn't usually insecure, I found myself listening to these leaders as they joked around and shared their experiences of youth ministry. I suddenly realized I didn't really have anything to say. After all, I was a youth myself— remember, I was just a senior in high school—and I barely knew enough about the Bible to share a devotional. During the services at the conference I began to wonder, "How in the world did I end up here?" My friends at home were probably off goofing around or playing sports.

I began to look for an exit. I had to get out of that place. It just wasn't for me. I remember going to my room one afternoon in total defeat. No one had really even spoken to me at the conference, and I was so out of place with all of the "qualified" who were there!

I made up my mind to go to one more evening service and then drive home. I would tell my pastor when I got home, "Sorry, you picked the wrong guy. Here are my church keys, and here is my resignation." That evening, as I walked toward the little chapel where the service was being held, I took a deep breath and stepped through the door. The guest speaker on stage was pastor Glen Berteau, a very well-known youth pastor. Glen had recently pastored the largest youth ministry in America in Baton Rouge, Louisiana. I was enamored with the anointing he carried.

I stood at the back door looking for an inconspicuous place to sit down so I could leave early. Then Glen began to say over and over these simple words: "God did not call you to fail." I listened to those words and fell to the floor weeping.

I realized that day that God could use me. I knew then God has the power to interrupt our self-driven doubts and insecurity because He has a plan bigger than we can imagine.

> "The unqualified is a human being so grossly lacking in his/her ability to accomplish a task and completely oblivious to its objective as defined by his fellow man that he finds himself stunned (as they are) by the perfect success which permeates his every Spirit-led move within a God-given task. It is this very human disqualification that uniquely qualifies him to be humbly, completely, and transparently used by God. It is only through those whose 'unqualification' cannot be denied that God's omnipotence is perfectly put on display."
>
> —Andy Oram, lay youth pastor, Albertville, AL

It doesn't matter what mistakes or failures from your past haunt your memory banks; God can still use you. Remember Romans 11:29: "God's gifts and God's call are under full warranty—never canceled, never rescinded" (THE MESSAGE).

Little did I know that later in life, Glen Berteau would become the greatest mentor and coach in my life. I did, however, pray that night as I drove home from the conference, "God, someday let that man become my friend." God is so cool that He did just that about seven years later!

Are You Available?

The purpose of this book is to help you realize that usually the most qualified are the ones who most often feel least qualified. They are the unqualified leaders of the qualifying God. Every person who has ever accepted the challenge to be used of God has at one time or another thought, "Why on earth, God, have You chosen me?" The question should instead be, "How could God *not* use me?"

In fact, we really have no right to question whether or not God can use us. Many years ago while spending time in prayer, I heard God say to me, "Pat, every time you doubt whether or not I can use you, it breaks My heart. It would be the same as you telling your children that you love them and them looking back at you and saying they don't believe you." That is how God feels when we doubt that He can use us.

The apostle Paul said it best:

> Who in the world do you think you are to second-guess God? Do you for one moment suppose any of us knows enough to call God into question? Clay doesn't talk back to the fingers that mold it, saying, "Why did you shape me like this?" Isn't it obvious that a potter has a perfect right to shape one lump of clay into a vase for holding flowers and another into a pot for cooking beans? If God needs one style of pottery especially designed to show his angry displeasure and another style carefully crafted to show his glorious goodness, isn't that all right? Either or both happens

to Jews, but it also happens to the other people. Hosea put it well: I'll call nobodies and make them some-bodies; I'll call the unloved and make them beloved. In the place where they yelled out, "You're nobody!" they're calling you "God's living children."
—ROMANS 9:20–26, THE MESSAGE

So many times when we see others blessed, we think God must play favorites. Surely others are in God's better graces than us! Let me be very clear when I say God doesn't play favorites. I am reminded of Simon Peter in Acts 10 as he ministered at the non-Jewish household of a man named Cornelius:

Peter fairly exploded with his good news: "It's God's own truth, nothing could be plainer: God plays no favorites! It makes no difference who you are or where you're from—if you want God and are ready to do as he says, the door is open. The Message he sent to the children of Israel—that through Jesus Christ every-thing is being put together again—well, he's doing it everywhere, among everyone."
—ACTS 10:34–36, THE MESSAGE

Peter let these Gentiles know the Spirit of God is for everyone. The door is open to everyone, and that means God can use anyone.

You're a survivor. All of Scripture proves that God uses the ones who most likely would not have been picked by man to be on His team of generals. Yet God is calling out to you. He refuses to leave you alone. Your scars are your testi-mony. The depth of God's love is most often revealed in the people least likely to be chosen in man's eyes. If you have been through lots of pain, then you're a great candidate to bring freedom to others.

It's just like the story of the precious sixteen-year-old girl I met in Indiana after a large youth convention. She came running up to me after I ministered and asked, "Can I talk to you?" I said, "Sure. How can I help you?" She had tears flowing down her face as she showed me her arms. She said, "I was raped by my dad, my stepdad, and my boyfriend, and I cut myself! But while you were preaching, the Lord told me to remove the Band-Aids from my arms that cover my scars. When I removed the Band-Aids, I noticed that God had healed all of my scars!" She began to dance around the foyer of that great convention center, praising God. She went on to say, "If God can heal my scars, then I can heal others!"

This was a girl who gets the heartbeat of what it means to be the unqualified. It's about knowing the pain of our past, trusting it to God, experiencing freedom and healing, then offering it up for God to use to set free and heal others too.

> "The unqualified are often overlooked and always underestimated. Their abilities are hidden by their humility and only truly exposed by the oppositions that they were created to conquer. They stand while everyone else bows. They step out while others hide. The unqualified rise while the more qualified fall."
>
> —Jayme Montera, international evangelist, Springfield, MO

What do you believe is the number one quality God uses to raise up people? Could it be their giftings—that if you're gifted enough, then you move to the top of the class for God's stage? I don't think so. Could it be your looks or stature? Honestly, I have seen some not-so-good-looking but very anointed people. Could it be who you know or your circle of friendships? I'm sure that helps some get through certain doors, but it will not keep them on the stage. Could it be the ones who are the most holy? No, we all have major flaws that we have to work on. Maybe a rich heritage, then? No, if that's the case, then I'm in trouble.

Do you remember the scripture I used to introduce this book? Here it is again:

> Take a good look, friends, at who you were when you got called into this life. I don't see many of "the brightest and the best" among you, not many influential, not many from high-society families. Isn't it obvious that God deliberately chose men and women that the culture overlooks and exploits and abuses, chose these "nobodies" to expose the hollow pretensions of the "somebodies"?
> —1 Corinthians 1:26–28, The Message

The scripture above tells us the main qualification in one word: *obedience.*

Have you ever noticed that right in the middle of the word *obedience* is the word *die*? Obedience means dying to everything, especially self.

Jesus is our example of obedience. His obedience set us free. Romans 5:19 states, "For just as through the disobedience of the one man the many were made sinners, so also through the obedience of the one man the many will be made righteous." I challenge you to show me one person who has lived a life of obedience to God who has not lived a completely fulfilling life. You can't do it.

God is calling each of us to lay down our own plans and agendas for the higher calling. It is through obedience that God is able to transform the nobodies. That means it's time to draw a line in the sand and walk away from the things that are holding you back. We are called to be empty vessels into which God can place His glory, and we better make sure we allow God to clean up these vessels that we are!

> But we have this treasure in earthen vessels, the excellency of the power being from God and not from ourselves.
> —2 Corinthians 4:7, mev

God needs empty, clean vessels. Don't ask God to use what He can't drink from! He promises to fill us if we are simply available.

> "The unqualified have one thing going for them that separates them from others, and that is their willingness to take a step when Jesus says, 'Follow Me.'"
>
> —Josh Wilbanks, youth pastor, Decatur, AL

It's time to realize that if God can use a kid from a small town who spent most of his early years getting in trouble and goofing off, then He can use you. Who was that kid? That would be me!

I will end this chapter with one of my favorite series of quotes that I have seen for years floating around the blogosphere. I have, in fact, shared this at gatherings where I have spoken. I call it "No More Excuses!"

> There are no excuses why God can't use you. The next time you think God can't use you, just look to the Bible to see what He had to work with:
> Noah was a drunk (Gen. 9:21).
> Abraham was too old (Gen. 17:17).
> Isaac was a daydreamer.
> Jacob was a liar (Gen. 27).
> Leah was ugly (Gen. 29:16–18).
> Joseph was abused (Gen. 37:22–28).
> Moses had a stuttering problem (Exod. 4:10).
> Gideon was afraid (Judg. 6).
> Samson had long hair and was a womanizer (Judg. 16:5, 17).
> Rahab was a harlot (Josh. 2:1).
> Jeremiah and Timothy were too young (Jer. 1:6).
> David had an affair and was a murderer (2 Sam. 11:2–4, 14–17).

Elijah was suicidal (1 Kings 19:4).
Isaiah preached naked (Isa. 20:2).
Jonah ran from God (Jon. 1:3).
Naomi was a widow (Ruth 1:3).
Job went bankrupt (Job 1:21).
Peter denied Christ (Mark 14:71).
The disciples fell asleep while praying (Matt. 26:40).
Martha worried about everything (Luke 10:40–42).
The Samaritan woman was divorced, more than
    once (John 4:17–18).
Zacchaeus was too small (Luke 19:2–3).
Paul was too religious.
Timothy had an ulcer (1 Tim. 5:23).
Lazarus was dead (John 11)![1]

As you can see, all of us have our issues. But God can use the unqualified to do great exploits. Remember, no more excuses!

"I have always felt unqualified, but I realize that I am not the one who needs to be qualified. It is God's perfect character that covers all of the areas where I am unqualified."

—Kalyn Schmidt, 18, ministry student, Hubbard, OH

Chapter 3

THE MESSIAH'S MISFITS

"The unqualified understand that the only reason they made it out of the depths of failure is because of the time spent at His feet."

—Rebekah Wright, 20,
ministry student, San Francisco, CA

G OD HAS NEVER asked you to be normal. God has called you to be different. What do I mean? God has never asked you to be a part of the world's system. Christianity is the greatest adventure you could ever take, and God is the greatest tour guide on this journey called the supernatural life for those of us who are unqualified. He will take you on a trip no human could have planned for you. Furthermore, the unqualified of God have never been called to fit in anyway. They are the ones man overlooks but God notices and plucks from obscurity!

There is one word that best describes the unqualified, and it is the word *misfit*. In fact, over and over the Bible reminds us that we are "strangers and pilgrims on the earth" (Heb. 11:13, MEV). We are even referred to as temporary residents who must watch our lives closely, as 1 Peter 2:11 states: "Dear friends, I warn you as 'temporary residents and foreigners' to keep away from worldly desires that wage war against your very souls" (NLT).

One of the greatest misconceptions is that very public

people have it all together. It is so easy to wear the mask of a "perfect Christian" when, really, under the mask is a person who has either fooled themselves with a false identity or relies so deeply on God that their cheeks are stained from hours of brokenness. The people God uses the most are the ones who realize they are nothing without Him.

Even so, society and culture do a great job of reminding Christians they don't fit in. We are living in a time where our value is so often determined by the number of friends we have on Facebook or the number of followers we have on Twitter. Society has a way of making us feel that our value is determined by how many people like us or how many followers we can get. For example, one day our family was talking about how many followers we all had on Instagram. My daughter, Abby, said to me jokingly, "Dad, if I can get six hundred followers, then I will be complete." Our whole family laughed at her statement. Nevertheless, society seriously places so much value on how many likes we can get or how many people will follow us.

> "The unqualified is a look into the mystery of why God uses the insignificant to accomplish the supernatural."
> —Daniel Haskett, youth pastor, Gastonia, NC

Our identity must not be determined by what the world says about us but by the fact that God dwells in us. But living this way makes us misfits.

It's certainly not the norm. And after a while, if you're not careful, the inner cry you have for God to use you can fade to a faint whisper of yesterday's promises. Instead, you must protect that cry and rise up and realize that as the unqualified, you are uniquely qualified to bring life to a lost world. God almost always chooses the one who wouldn't get picked to be on man's team to be an all-star on God's team.

Proverbs 15:25 says, "God smashes the pretensions of the arrogant; he stands with those who have no standing" (THE MESSAGE).

From One Misfit to Another

To share my own misfit story with you, let me say that no matter how hard I have tried, I have never been able to fit in. Believe me, I have absolutely tried. In high school and college I tried to run with the crowd. After all, that was the path of least resistance. But even then there were times— even while I was in the midst of sin—when God would awaken me to the fact that He was right there calling to me.

I would even have dreams of preaching the gospel when I abhorred the very thought of it. I have often said that the best way to know whether or not you are called is that you go to bed thinking about it, you wake up thinking about it, and everything that happens to you would be a great sermon illustration. That was my life. Even while running as fast as I could from God and His plan, I still thought about Him all the time. And God will drive you crazy until you finally give in. He is a jealous God (Exod. 34:14).

I wish I could say I was always on fire for God, but that is just not the truth. The truth of the matter is that if you had met me in high school, you would have never believed that someday I would be a minister, author, or anything else. I guess you could say I was headed for a life of pain.

It wasn't that I got in a lot of trouble, but I was definitely rebellious. I lived on the fringe. I knew just enough Christianese to keep the religious guessing and enough trash talk to keep the world from guessing. In fact, I hated everything that had to do with religion. I guess you could say I was in full-blown rebellion toward my parents, the church, and most of all my Creator. I had felt for so long that if God was truly a God of love and freedom, then why did it seem the religious were so miserable and the righteous so misunderstood? This was also a time where I saw my parents persecuted for their stands for righteousness, and that made my argument against the church all the more potent.

Now here is the problem. If you ever have a true encounter with God, then it will ruin you. You see, I had experienced God on many occasions in my early years. There were times in my younger years that I would get so overwhelmed by God. And when God comes near, it changes everything around you. I knew what the psalmist meant when he wrote, "You make known to me the path of life; you will fill me with joy in your presence, with eternal pleasures at your right hand" (Ps. 16:11). I knew God was always only a whisper away. There were times as a young boy I could literally feel God in the atmosphere.

> "I'm just an unqualified scarlet woman with a big red S for scarlet branded on my entire body, because of unbelievable insanity at times! Then the blood of Jesus turned the S on my being into a big S for saved and it is written in crimson red that flowed over my entire being inside and out. It is because of Jesus I'm qualified! He loves me!"
>
> —Dr. Deb Schatzline (the author's mom), cofounder of Daystar Ministries International, Northport, AL

I remember one particular season around the age of twelve when God would visit my bedroom at night. That season of life was very tough, because my precious mom had experienced a mental breakdown from the pressures of ministry and life. She went away to a hospital for two weeks to get things back together. During that time of deep pain I knew that God was close by. I would fall asleep talking to Him. It was during this time of my life that I continually read Psalm 91. God would later heal my mom, and things were restored in a powerful way in our home.

Then life happened and peer pressure became a very large stronghold in my life. Our family lived in a very religious southern culture, where Christianity came with one's breeding, but those with a deep walk with God were considered Jesus freaks. I strayed far away from God. Bitterness crept in because of all that had happened in our family. I blamed people in the church and most of all God for some things that had hurt our family. I bought into the lie that God only blessed certain people. To make matters worse, I was now running from the only One who could have freed me.

Nevertheless, God would not leave me alone. I've found that God will make you absolutely miserable until you submit to His plan. It seemed as if every direction I went, He was standing there, calling out to me. Part of me enjoyed what the world had to offer, but another part of me so deeply wanted to experience God at another level.

Then late one night while camping with some high school friends during my junior year, I had a supernatural experience. That night my friends and I had been drinking alcohol. In fact, we were drinking a homemade concoction called hunch punch. To this day I am not sure what went into this soup of intoxication, but I will tell you the after burn was no fun.

After hanging out with my friends for a while, I decided to go for a walk alone in a nearby field. I still remember how bright the moon and stars were that night as I sat down on the ground and lay back on a tree trunk.

Suddenly as I lay there, I saw the clouds roll back and the face of Jesus appear. I know that sounds crazy, but even then God did things to get my attention that some may call spectacular. Nevertheless, as the clouds rolled back, I saw the face of Jesus and then saw a tear roll down that face.

As I stared at it, I instantly sobered up. It seemed like an eternity as I looked upon His face. I thought, "Surely my friends see this too." But of course they didn't.

Then I saw Jesus turn His back, and the vision was over.

I began to shake. I knew that I had to change. I knew time was running out. In fact, it was during this season of my life that I experienced many supernatural events that forced change in my life.

People often ask me why I don't drink alcohol now, and the answer is simple. I can't go back to what Christ freed me from. Why would I want to be a slave to what has destroyed so many of the unqualified? The freedom we experienced at the cross requires that we make a stand. I have even been called religious by some Christians who indulge in alcohol, but I would rather be considered religious than be in rehab. I can never go back to what could have destroyed me.

I share that story because I realized through it that I was never called to fit into this world. I must be different. If God can visit me in a field in rural Alabama, I figured maybe He could use me as His vessel after all. After receiving Christ as Savior and Lord a few weeks later, I made up my mind to never be religious and, most of all, to never fit in. If we can be radical for the world, then why can't we be misfits for our Savior?

Normal is boring. We are called to be different. Your testimony is proof that God never gave up on you. The mistakes of yesterday that brought you great shame will someday be used as a praise report.

What happened to me in that field many years ago was never shared publicly until many years after I went into the ministry. Why? Because we are often told to let our past be our past. Yet I believe it is when we share the miraculous grace of our Lord Jesus that we step further into victory and also give others permission to get free. Revelation 12:11 says, "They triumphed over him [Satan] by the blood of the Lamb *and by the word of their testimony*; they did not love their lives so much as to shrink from death" (emphasis added).

Never be ashamed of what you've survived! For one thing, your scars scare Satan. They are proof you survived when he thought you wouldn't make it. But even more, if your past is full of failures and God's grace interrupted your mistakes, don't run from your story. The Holy Spirit stuck with you because He could see where you would someday be. Let your story be your wings that help you soar to great heights with God!

I believe with all my heart that if I had chosen to walk the way of the religious instead of the way of the crucified, then I would have remained just as miserable as a Christian as I was as a sinner. God has called us to live an outlandish life of devil-kicking, freedom-loving, supernatural encounters with our Savior. This journey we are on with our King should never be boring.

> "I would rather be considered unqualified, because then it is no longer about what I can do but what He can do through me!"
>
> —Tommy Vardaman, 20, ministry student, Portage, IN

Still Need Convincing?

In 1 Corinthians 4 the apostle Paul gets radically real about the importance of this misfit life. He lived in a time when Christians were under great persecution by the Jewish religious leaders and the sectarian government of Rome. Because of the attacks from every direction, Christians were seeking out identity. Different sects were being formed, and many of the new Christians were posturing for position and man's approval. Paul writes the church at Corinth and confronts man's concepts. He reminds everyone that we must be servants and guides:

> Don't imagine us leaders to be something we aren't. We are servants of Christ, not his masters. We are guides into God's most sublime secrets, not security guards posted to protect them. The requirements for a good guide are reliability and accurate knowledge. It matters very little to me what you think of me, even less where I rank in popular opinion. I don't even rank myself. Comparisons in these matters are pointless. I'm not aware of anything that would disqualify me from being a good guide for you, but that doesn't mean much. The Master makes that judgment.
> —1 CORINTHIANS 4:1–4, THE MESSAGE

Paul was instructing the Corinthians to quit looking at him and look at God. Can you imagine the responses from the pompous religious after they got their hands on this letter? It challenges the religious establishment and reduces "the called" to being servants. This would mean that people would no longer lift them up as a statue, bow to the cloth, and chase after their approval. Paul even said he didn't think he was qualified as their leader but, really, God is the only One who can make that call. Then Paul tells us the truth about what it means to be in God's holy army:

> It seems to me that God has put us who bear his Message on stage in a theater in which no one wants to buy a ticket. We're something everyone stands around and stares at, like an accident in the street. *We're the Messiah's misfits.* You might be sure of yourselves, but we live in the midst of frailties and uncertainties. You might be well-thought-of by others, but we're mostly kicked around. Much of the time we don't have enough to eat, we wear patched and threadbare clothes, we get doors slammed in our faces, and we pick up odd jobs anywhere we can to eke out a

living. When they call us names, we say, "God bless
you." When they spread rumors about *us*, we put in a
good word for *them*. We're treated like garbage, potato
peelings from the culture's kitchen. And it's not getting any better.

—1 CORINTHIANS 4:9–10, THE MESSAGE,
EMPHASIS ADDED

I absolutely love this. We're on a stage no one wants to see!
We're an accident in the streets! We're the misfits! Throughout
history God has always used the least likely and the most
unqualified to provoke change. These are His misfits.

The word *misfit* means "a person who is not suited or is
unable to adjust to the circumstances of his or her particular
situation."[1] The Urban Dictionary says, "Misfits tend to follow
their own beliefs, and are usually persecuted for it."[2] If that's
the case, then the Bible is full of misfits—those who usually lost out on man's approval but always won with a God-
dreamed vision.

Today those going into ministry sometimes have a different concept of the ministry. It tends to be about numbers,
crowds, sizes, who you know, where you've been, and the
names you're associated with. Many times it can be about
pleasing a denomination, making a big salary, or flowing
with the newest concept—but don't fool yourself. Just be
willing to be used with no preconceived notions about how
God will use you.

Don't fool yourself. Don't think that you can be wise
merely by being up-to-date with the times. Be God's
fool—that's the path to true wisdom. What the world
calls smart, God calls stupid. It's written in Scripture,
He exposes the chicanery of the chic. The Master sees
through the smoke screens of the know-it-alls.

—1 CORINTHIANS 3:18–20, THE MESSAGE

God Uses the Salty Folks

When we look at the birth of the New Testament church, it wasn't the well-dressed, educated, and proper religious leaders who led the way from the Upper Room to rest of the world. No, it was a bunch of fishermen. Like, for instance, have you ever watched the TV show *The Deadliest Catch*? That is a rough and tough bunch of people—and that is exactly what the majority of the disciples were like when Jesus interrupted their lives. It's easy to watch Bible-based movies and think those who portray the disciples and even Jesus are good-looking models holding a rods and reels, but actually these men were weathered and uncouth. They hadn't received any formal training or taken any classes on public etiquette. Really, they were blue-collared rednecks—just a group of guys who would become fishers of men! Jesus spoke their language on the day He called them by saying, "Follow Me, and I will make you fishers of men" (Matt. 4:19, MEV).

Now look at this account of Peter and John praying for the lame man in Acts 3. The Bible says that one day when they were going to pray at the temple, they saw the beggar at the Gate Beautiful. This man had been lame his entire life. The beggar asked Peter and John for some money. These misfits didn't have any money, but what they possessed was better than money. They possessed a power from above.

Acts 3:6–8 gives this account:

> Then Peter said, "I have no silver and gold, but I give you what I have. In the name of Jesus Christ of Nazareth, rise up and walk." He took him by the right hand and raised him up. Immediately his feet and ankles were strengthened. Jumping up, he stood and walked and entered the temple with them, walking and jumping and praising God.
>
> —MEV

"God loves the least, last, and lost. It shouldn't surprise us that He handpicks the foolish to confound the wise. Those that were rejected locally often are promoted by God globally for His glory. Being unqualified is greater than a degree from an Ivy League school. Graduate with God today because the Lord doesn't call the qualified but qualifies the called."

—Frank Shelton, author *Carrying Greatness*, Fox News contributor, and evangelism chairman of the 2012 Olympics outreach

This miracle shocked the people and irritated the religious, but the people looked on with wonder. I imagine they thought to themselves that these guys were superheroes. Remember, this was the first public miracle to take place after the death and resurrection of Jesus.

This was the moment Peter and John could have soaked in the adoration of the people. Maybe they could have even hired a public relations team to handle all of the speaking requests, interviews, and future crusades that were sure to come their way. Instead, Peter pushed against the people's perceptions. He let them know he and John weren't superheroes:

> As the lame man who was healed held on to Peter and John, all the people ran together to them in the entrance that is called Solomon's Porch, greatly amazed. When Peter saw it, he answered the people: "Men of Israel, why do you marvel at this man? Or why do you stare at us, as if by our own power or piety we had made him walk? The God of Abraham and Isaac and Jacob, the God of our fathers, has glorified His Son Jesus, whom you handed over and denied in the presence of Pilate, when he had decided to release Him. You denied the Holy and Righteous One and asked for

> a murderer to be granted to you, and you killed the
> Creator of Life, whom God has raised from the dead,
> of which we are witnesses. And His name, by faith in
> His name, has made this man strong, whom you see
> and know. And faith which comes through Him has
> given him perfect health in your presence."
>
> —Acts 3:11–16, mev

Peter further used this miraculous moment to remind the people that they had helped crucify Jesus. Remember, this was the same very flawed misfit Simon Peter who had fallen asleep in the garden the night Jesus was betrayed. This was the same misfit guy who cut off the ear of the high priest's soldier. And who can forget this was the same guy who betrayed Jesus as the rooster crowed? This was simply a man so flawed that, without God, he was hopelessly lost.

In fact, Peter even tried to go back to his old life after failing! That's right—Simon Peter resigned the ministry. He quit. In John 21:3 he said, "I am going fishing!" That only lasted for one night, because the next morning Jesus was waiting on the shore with breakfast.

As you can see, God even uses quitters. He uses the ones who fail, curse, betray, and quit. He uses the ones who have quit trying to be something they're not and simply allow themselves to be God's vessel through which God channels His power. He really does use the unqualified.

This is why I like Simon Peter so much. I can't tell you how many times I've wanted to quit and walk away too. Yet the next morning I usually saw Jesus on the shore, telling me the same thing He told Peter: "If you love Me, feed my sheep." (See John 21:17.) How can we quit on the Lamb who has called us to feed His lambs?

We cannot quit! We must hold on. Our mantra must be Galatians 6:9: "Let us not become weary in doing good, for at the proper time we will reap a harvest if we do not give up." If circumstances, people, or lack can cause us to quit so easily on a Father who promised to never leave us or forsake us, then we haven't taken the Great Commission seriously enough. Our victory is not found in what we accomplish, but rather in our ability to never stop chasing God's awesome calling. I once heard someone say, "If the cost is too great, then the call is not enough!" I must take it one step further and say that if you're able to accomplish your dream on your own, then God never birthed the dream you're following.

> "The Bible says in Acts 4:13, 'When they saw the boldness of Peter and John, they perceived they were untrained and uneducated men, they marveled. And they realized they had been with Jesus.' The unqualified are individuals who are willing to let the world see who they are not so they can see who they have been with!"
>
> —James Levesque, pastor, New London, CT

Will They Know You've Been With Jesus?

Remember, you're bound to be a misfit when you're following God's call. Peter and John found themselves in trouble for walking in the miraculous immediately after healing that man. I've found that when people don't understand the supernatural power of God, they always put God's vessels on trial to defend what they've never experienced. In Acts 4:13 it says, "When they saw the courage of Peter and John and realized that they were unschooled, ordinary men, they were astonished and they took note that these men had been with Jesus."

What made these unqualified servants of Jesus stand out as they went about preaching the gospel was not who they were but who they knew. The neon sign lit over their lives said these men had been with Jesus. You must understand that would not mean they'd be celebrated. No, they were abused, isolated, taunted, flogged, imprisoned, and martyred for this rebel named Jesus Christ. What was it that made these men so special? They understood that without God's intervention in their lives, they were simply unqualified fools.

> "The unqualified are poor and needy—nothing more than an island of misfits. That's who God picks! They have found that nothing in the world is of interest—their only interest is in living a life sold out to the kingdom of God. They are often hidden behind the closed doors, calling out for the revival fire of conviction for holiness and repentance followed with living in obedience and reverence to kingdom authority. They do not consult with flesh and blood but instead run to the Holy Spirit to proclaim Jesus with a thundering from their heart."
>
> —Ruth Anna Spitsbergen, pastor, San Diego, CA

Do you know what made these men so feared by the religious and powerful in the kingdom of God? It really is simple. They never relied on themselves to do anything. Their entire reputation was one that made others sit up and say, "These guys have been with Jesus!" They continually pointed back to Him.

The apostle Paul reiterated this same reality:

> You'll remember, friends, that when I first came to you to let you in on God's master stroke, I didn't try to impress you with polished speeches and the latest philosophy. I deliberately kept it plain and simple: first Jesus and who he is; then Jesus and what he did— Jesus crucified. I was unsure of how to go about this, and felt totally inadequate—I was scared to death, if you want the truth of it—and so nothing I said could have impressed you or anyone else. But the Message

came through anyway. God's Spirit and God's power did it, which made it clear that your life of faith is a response to God's power, not to some fancy mental or emotional footwork by me or anyone else.
—1 Corinthians 2:1–5, The Message

As the unqualified, we must desire that when people walk away from us, they never see us but Jesus. If people see Jesus instead of you, they may actually follow Him and not just you on Twitter and Instagram.

It's like what I heard from the Lord one time as I got ready to speak at a rather large event. I was standing off stage waiting to be introduced when God said, "Pat, be My stagehand tonight! Lift the curtain and let Me shine. If people can see you, then they can't see Me. If they can see Me, then they won't see you!"

> "God turns the normal into an anomaly and calls the unqualified to stand up for truth, not fearing what people would say about them but fearing what God would say about them."
>
> —Christina Sacra, 21, ministry student, Chesterfield, VA

Again, I have often thought, "God, how could You use me?" And I then realized I must always additionally pray, "Oh, God, never let me use You for my own gain!" The moment we spotlight ourselves, we let people down and tarnish the kingdom of God.

God's Power, Not Ours

If God can use Simon Peter, then He can use you and me. But if ever we think we can accomplish anything without God's help, then we have bought a lie that leads to destruction.

If you wonder where the power of God has gone, you need only to look at the mainstream Christian messages that flood the airwaves with overinflated egos espousing self-help sermons, watered-down talks, and hyper-grace theology. Eloquent speech and cool clothes have never chased a demon out of anyone. When we reduce preaching down to an art that doesn't require Spirit unction and Spirit visitation, then God simply becomes a late-night infomercial that lulls us to sleep.

To preach a compromising gospel that doesn't require repentance makes us no different from the religious who sell indulgences and penance. We are living in a day where nice messages and sweet services simply allow the demons to relax and make fodder of God's people. When we place God in a box of human rationality, we only experience human results. William Booth prophesied over a hundred years ago a message that speaks to our present day. He said, "I consider that the chief dangers which confront the coming century will be religion without the Holy Ghost, Christianity without Christ, forgiveness without repentance, salvation without regeneration, politics without God, and heaven without hell."[3]

This is exactly why God is awakening the misfits—the unqualified! I believe purity is the backbone of authority, and authority is determined by brokenness. The spiritual depth of the unqualified will not come from degrees on the wall or memberships in prestigious God clubs but from the classroom of brokenness. We are living in perilous times that require every God-ordained misfit to crawl back to the closet of brokenness and walk out endued with power from on high. Our prayer must be Psalm 51:17: "The sacrifices of God are a broken spirit; a broken and a contrite heart, O God, You will not despise" (MEV). If you will cry out on your knees in your prayer closet, then you will stand on the shoulders of God in the public square.

> "The unqualified are fearless. They have nothing to lose because He had nothing to prove in the first place. Everything they do is purely for the glory of God. They are eternally grateful because they never knew that they had a place in the game. But one day God chooses them and brings them into this special remnant called the unqualified."
>
> —Paul Liu Jiancong, youth pastor, Singapore

God has anointed you for now. No more excuses! All through the Bible we see God raise up the unqualified. These are the ones no one saw coming. These are even the ones who had great flaws in their armor. Whether it was Noah, Moses, or David, when they came on the scene, everyone had their doubts. Yet God has always confounded the wise. He doesn't look for social stature, good looks, or even the most intellectual among us. He calls forth the available, no matter how misfitting they are.

Chapter 4

YOU ARE NOT PLAN B

"It is the unqualified that no one ever thought or believed would be successful by following the calling of the Lord but yet rises above the voices of doubt, fear, and insecurities to see the Lord use them uniquely."

—Jamie Kowalski, minister, Birmingham, AL

M Y GREATEST WORRY as you read this book is that you'll gather the perception that being the unqualified means you are God's plan B or His second choice. One of the greatest lies from the enemy is that you and I are indeed second best or plan B—that God will maybe use us eventually if He can't find someone else. But God is not a God who says, "Well, on second thought," as if He is stuck using someone because others weren't available. If that were the case, God would not be a very good father, as one of the greatest qualities of a good dad is his ability to never choose favorites. Only when we understand God is a *great* father do we become candidates for a "What's next, Papa?" moment.

> This resurrection life you received from God is not a timid, grave-tending life. It's adventurously expectant, greeting God with a childlike "What's next, Papa?" God's Spirit touches our spirits and confirms who we really are. We know who he is, and we know who we are: Father and children. And we know we are going to

> get what's coming to us—an unbelievable inheritance!
> We go through exactly what Christ goes through. If we
> go through the hard times with him, then we're cer-
> tainly going to go through the good times with him!
> —ROMANS 8:15–17, THE MESSAGE

This plan B concept is a major part of our society, though. We use this term if our original plans fail. It's used in politics, sports, and even concerning unborn children. In fact, it's an actual name for a type of contraception taken as a pill after unprotected sex to stop a pregnancy, also known as the "morning-after pill."

I wrote about this pill in my book *I Am Remnant.* The holocaust of the unborn in our nation is described in a chapter called "The Massacre of the Innocents," where I spoke of a federal judge who "ordered the Food and Drug Administration to make the 'morning-after' pill available without prescription to girls of all ages within one month."[1] This means that a child can now walk into a store and buy an abortion pill but not allergy medicine. Clearly we live in a day where plan B is the alternative when our original plan doesn't work out.

But just as an unborn child is not a plan B, neither are you or I. We are a part of God's perfect plan. You are not an afterthought; you are a part of the original vision. This is an absolute fact, but we must also realize that God needs us to accomplish His plans: "We humans keep brainstorming options and plans, but GOD's purpose prevails" (Prov. 19:21, THE MESSAGE).

Once again here is the prophetic word God gave me when I began to write this book:

> Pat, I will use the unqualified to awaken the qualified
> out of their drunken stupor that has been caused by
> the intoxication of self-built kingdoms. These man-
> made kingdoms have been built upon the sand of
> shifting truth and a forfeited authority. The unquali-
> fied will be the ones that confound the very concept

of what we have called the qualified for many generations. It's the oops, the accidents, and the nobodies
that will rise up and take the place of those who have
grown comfortable with the idea of maintenance faith
versus miraculous faith. Let Me be very clear: You are
not plan B. You are the valued of the Lord!

God decided to use you because He's already declared your
days. You are not here to just fill space and exist. You are
here to take dominion and walk in the supernatural power
of God! There will be those who fall away or don't accept
the mandate God has on their lives. There will be those who
walk away from the call of God and His amazing love.

> But you walked away from your first love—why?
> What's going on with you, anyway? Do you have any
> idea how far you've fallen? A Lucifer fall! Turn back!
> Recover your dear early love. No time to waste, for
> I'm well on my way to removing your light from the
> golden circle.
> —REVELATION 2:4–5, THE MESSAGE

The thing is, God knows in advance they will fall or walk
away. When that happens—at that moment—God then uses
others. That doesn't make those others He uses a plan B.
Rather, it makes them a case of planned obedience!

I'm sure you've seen this in action. People make decisions
that harm their calling, and then it appears a door opens
for someone else to fill the void. The fact is that God knew
that first person was going to fall away or make bad choices.
When they decide to walk away from the plan of God, God
already has someone in place to fill the void.

I've learned even more about this through the example of
one of my heroes, evangelist Reinhard Bonnke. One of my
favorite stories Reinhard tells is what happened when God
called him to a life of evangelism. He speaks easily about
a dialogue they had. It seems God laid out for him what

would be expected. Reinhard told God he would obey and follow what God was asking of him. Before this extended conversation ended, however, God told him, "You weren't My first choice." Reinhard listened. "You weren't My second choice either."

Later on when there was a time Reinhard hesitated to schedule a specific crusade, he says he wavered and then God said, "You drop the vision and I drop you."[2] God let him know there were others He had originally planned to use, but they wouldn't take up the mantle God had for them. Therefore, God chose Reinhard to carry it—and if Reinhard refused to carry it, God had someone else in mind for that too.

Another dear friend named Pastor Jim Hennesy, pastor of Trinity Church in Cedar Hill, Texas, once told me, "I wasn't the first choice on the list of pastors for the church. In fact, I was number three on the list." Jim and Becky have led the church into two major building projects, and the church now has thousands of members who encounter God every week. Were these great leaders plan B or even plan C? No, they were the ones who accepted the call!

> "Your choice concerning me carries no weight over His choice in choosing me! The fact that there is breath in my lungs is God's signature on my life that I am chosen! I am unqualified!"
>
> —Josh Carter, international evangelist, North Carolina

When we're available to be used by God, the sky is the limit. God has always raised up the available. He doesn't go looking for the most gifted or talented to fill a void. What we often forget is that we are made of clay. He shapes us into what He desires. He never exalts the arrogant and haughty. He uses those who are humble and available.

I'm Not Plan B Either

"Everyone has flaws in their armor. As a leader, you have to find your flaws and allow God to fix your armor."

Those are the words of a dear friend who believed in me years ago. His name was Pastor Jerry Parritt. In my first book, *Why Is God So Mad at Me?*, I listed him as one of the voices that most greatly influenced my life.

In truth, the day I met Jerry would forever change my life. I was between my sophomore and junior years of college at Southeastern College (now Southeastern University) in Lakeland, Florida. I had decided to stay in college through the summer to try and knock out some courses. I lived in a small apartment off campus with a couple of roommates.

One Friday, June 29, 1990, my roommates and I had decided to go to the beach for the day. As we were getting ready, though, I heard the voice of the Lord say to me, "Pat, stay home and pray today."

I tried to ignore the voice and continued to load the car for the beach trip. Then I heard it again: "Pat, stay home and pray today."

I was overwhelmed. I had never felt anything like this. I finally turned to my friends and said, "Guys, I have to stay home and pray." They thought I was joking at first, but as I walked back to the apartment they realized I was serious.

Throughout the morning I lay on the floor listening to the only worship tape that I owned. I must say that I can still remember the stirring in my heart. During my prayer time I asked the Lord if He could use me. As I prayed, in my mind's eye I saw thousands and thousands of lost teenagers in need of hope.

Finally, at about 1:00 or 2:00 p.m., I heard a knock at the door. I walked over and opened the door, and there stood a man in his late forties with piercing blue eyes and a gregarious smile.

I know he must have seen my tear-stained face because I had just gotten up off the floor from praying.

He said, "Hello, my name is Pastor Jerry Parritt. Is Pat Schatzline home?"

I said, "Yes, sir. That's me."

He went on to say the college had given him four names to talk with concerning his desire to hire a youth pastor at the church he pastored in Durant, Florida. The church, Pleasant Grove Assembly of God, was about sixty miles from Lakeland, near Tampa.

He said, "I tried the first three guys and they weren't home. You're the last one on my list. Would you like to take a ride out to Durant?"

I said, "Yes, sir! Let's go!"

Six days later on July 4, 1990, I became the youth pastor of Pleasant Grove Assembly of God. That church is the place I saw God do great things in the lives of many students, but most of all in my life.

Just two months later Karen and I were married, and we lived in a little parsonage on the property. Two years after that we left Durant to pursue other places of ministry, but Jerry and Carol Parritt had become a mom and dad to Karen and me. Throughout the years they have been the two we've called on again and again for wisdom and advice.

Why did I share this story? The answer is simple. I wasn't the first name on the list to be interviewed. In fact, I was the fourth name on the list! Pastor Parritt had tried the other three, but none of them were at home that day. The only one at home was a kid who heard the voice of God say, "Pat, stay home and pray today."

I could have gotten offended that I was the last on the list. I could have asked, "Why was I last?" Nope! I was just happy the knock came on the door at all. Remember, I'd just been asking God if He could use me. It turns out, I wasn't last on the list in God's plan. I was the one who heeded His voice. I'm not sure who the other guys on the list were, but the name at the end got the assignment. The truth is, God never called us to be first on the list. He's simply called us to be *on* the list.

Five Things to Remember When You're Feeling Like Plan B

Here are five guidelines for the unqualified to keep in mind, especially when tempted to feel like plan B.

1. Remember God rescued you.

When you're keenly aware God is the one who began the work in your life, you will not trip over the lies of the enemy. God chose to rescue you regardless of where you were in your life. God knew where you were!

> Some of you were locked in a dark cell, cruelly con-
> fined behind bars, punished for defying God's Word,
> for turning your back on the High God's counsel—a
> hard sentence, and your hearts so heavy, and not a
> soul in sight to help. Then you called out to GOD in
> your desperate condition; he got you out in the nick
> of time. He led you out of your dark, dark cell, broke
> open the jail and led you out. So thank GOD for his
> marvelous love, for his miracle mercy to the children
> he loves; he shattered the heavy jailhouse doors, he
> snapped the prison bars like matchsticks!
> —PSALM 107:10–16, THE MESSAGE

2. Remember you don't have the right to question the call of God.

Your calling isn't by chance! The call of God is often defined as a God encounter that took place at an altar experience or a moment where the light came on. It is not so easily defined, however. The call of God comes after our submission to the cross, our death to self, and, most important of all, our abandonment of all future plans. Be faithful where you are planted.

Think too of how God has raised up leaders:

- Moses was pasturing the flock of Jethro, his father-in-law.
- Elijah was a farmer.
- David was tending sheep for his father.
- Esther was a concubine.
- Jacob was a slave.
- Peter was a fisherman.
- Luke was a doctor.
- Paul was a tentmaker.
- The Lord Himself was a carpenter.

They were faithful to where they started, and then God called them out.

> We are intimately linked in this harvest work. Anyone who accepts what you do, accepts me, the One who sent you. Anyone who accepts what I do accepts my Father, who sent me. Accepting a messenger of God is as good as being God's messenger. Accepting someone's help is as good as giving someone help. This is a large work I've called you into, but don't be overwhelmed by it. It's best to start small. Give a cool cup of water to someone who is thirsty, for instance. The smallest act of giving or receiving makes you a true apprentice. You won't lose out on a thing.
> —Matthew 10:40–42, The Message

3. Remember your calling will always be something of a mystery.

God has called you to enjoy the mystery of His call. Paul called the plan of God a mystery (Eph. 1:9–10). The word *mystery* in the Greek is *musterion* (moos-tay'-ree-on) and is "from a derivative of *muo* (to shut the mouth); a secret or 'mystery' (through the idea of silence imposed by initiation into religious rites)."[3]

Make sure you understand that in your quest for the high call, the mystery keeps it fresh. You must remain silent about your mystery; in other words, don't try to explain what God has done in you. You will never be able to explain why you have chosen this path to those who have not accepted the call. The death of explanation will bring forth a life of miracles. It is truly impossible to explain a life of consecration to the highest call in the land.

In truth, I have spent most of my ministry in the dark! And I know I'm not the only one who can say this. But the mystery of what's next has always forced me to chase after God and enjoy the journey.

To those who are called, you need to understand:

- You will spend many days wondering what is next.
- You will spend many nights weeping for those you lost.
- You will run to pain and flee from compromise.
- You will be asked to serve when you are tired.

Just remember it is all about the mystery.

> Making known to us the mystery of His will, according to His good pleasure, which He purposed in Himself, as a plan for the fullness of time, to unite all things in Christ, which are in heaven and on earth.
> —EPHESIANS 1:9–10, MEV

4. Remember the enemy is after your anointing.

The devil is jealous of what he lost, so his goal is to torture the saints and reduce the called. It is sad to say, but he is winning. If we don't understand what the anointing does in and through our lives, we will abuse it or let it be abused.

Jesus never called you to drink the anointing oil but to wear it. We must guard the anointing!

> This is exactly what Christ promised: eternal life, real life! I've written to warn you about those who are trying to deceive you. But they're no match for what is embedded deeply within you—Christ's anointing, no less! You don't need any of their so-called teaching. Christ's anointing teaches you the truth on everything you need to know about yourself and him, uncontaminated by a single lie. Live deeply in what you were taught.
> —1 John 2:25–27, The Message

5. Remember you are meant to lose your rights.

Every one of us battles with protecting our image. Nevertheless, the self loses its value when we go to prayer. The only image we are called to protect is the image of God. Colossians 4:2–6 advises us:

> Devote yourselves to prayer, being watchful and thankful. And pray for us, too, that God may open a door for our message, so that we may proclaim the mystery of Christ, for which I am in chains. Pray that I may proclaim it clearly, as I should. Be wise in the way you act toward outsiders; make the most of every opportunity. Let your conversation be always full of grace, seasoned with salt, so that you may know how to answer everyone.

When you and I vote in an election, we are exercising our rights as citizens. So when you de-vote, you're losing your rights. The apostle Paul says everything starts with prayer. He goes on to say that when you start with prayer, you will know how to handle yourself in public. When I went into ministry, I thought God needed my voice, and now I know I must hear His.

> "The Unqualified is someone that feels lost, hurt, abandoned, and useless. God uses your healing in these areas as a connection point for others feeling the same way! God will use your greatest weaknesses in the world as your greatest strengths in His kingdom!"
>
> —Elisa Roberts, evangelist, entrepreneur, and ministry student, Midlothian, TX

The Door Is Open to You

The last time I spoke with Jerry Parritt was on Tuesday, August 24, 2014. I was about to board a flight to Singapore and felt compelled to call him from the airport. He was in the hospital battling an aggressive form of cancer, and I wanted him to know I loved him. As we got ready to end the call, I said, "Pastor, you're my hero!" He said, "Well, I am proud of you, and I love you!" I then promised to come and see him a couple weeks later when I would be in Frankfort, Kentucky, where he lived. He passed away before I ever got to talk to him again.

I was honored to be one of four speakers at Pastor Parritt's funeral on September 15, 2014. The church was standing room only as family, friends, and mostly ministers came from all over to honor his life. The funeral was a celebration of a man who loved people regardless of their past. He simply knew how to love and encourage everyone.

During the funeral service I shared the story about the day he knocked at my door in the summer of 1990 and how he had taken a chance on a young kid who needed a start in ministry.

A few nights later I had a very powerful dream. In the dream I heard a knock at the door. When I answered the door, there stood Jerry Parritt again. This time a bright light shone around him, and he looked younger than when I had first met him. No longer was his body worn out and eaten up with cancer. No, there he stood with the glory of the Lord all around him.

I remember weeping as I embraced him. We hugged as he stood in the doorway, and I knew that I was looking into heaven. He smiled and said, "Pat, I wouldn't come back if I could! Heaven is glorious. I came to tell you that I am cheering you on in heaven!"

Then suddenly a woman burst past him into the room. She was dark skinned and spoke with an African accent. She ran past me and then looked back and said, "We are all cheering you on! The nations must be won to the Father!" Then she ran out the door and the door shut. After that I woke up.

I learned from this dream that God has a door waiting for the obedient. It doesn't matter how you perceive yourself. It doesn't matter what mistakes you've made. Answer the door and walk through, past the threshold of doubt. God is always waiting for you. It is the promise of Revelation 3:8: "I know your deeds. See, I have placed before you an open door that no one can shut. I know that you have little strength, yet you have kept my word and have not denied my name."

You're Always God's First Choice

I'll end this refutation of the plan B notion by telling you a story about my little girl. She came to us from God via China. For many years we tried to have another child but to no avail; my wife could not get pregnant again. In a dream my wife could hear a child crying out for her. Then the Lord told us to go to China. Abby was nine months old when she joined our family in October 2003.

The process of adoption is not an easy one. It takes a great deal of work, which includes home studies, lots of paperwork, and a large amount of finances. What many do not realize is that in the process of adopting Abby, our plans were put on hold by a disease called SARS (severe acute respiratory syndrome). This disease spread throughout Asia from 2002–2003.[4] We watched it closely but were told over and over it would not affect our adoption. We checked the mail every day for our final paperwork telling us to come get our daughter, and then everything stopped.

On Friday, May 16, 2003, I flew to Eau Claire, Wisconsin, to speak at a youth conference. While checking into the hotel, I saw the *New York Times* in a newspaper stand. I reached over to grab the paper and my heart suddenly sank. The paper had these words on the front page: "China Suspends Adoptions and Sets Edict to Fight SARS."[5]

> "It is the unqualified that must, at all cost, step into the greatness God has designed for them despite the world's cruel condemnation."
>
> —Maegan Fleming, 18, student, Chesterfield, VA

I immediately called Karen back home to see if she had seen or heard the news. She hadn't. Our hearts were broken, and we wept on the phone. We were so close to going to get our daughter, and now a terrible disease stood in the way.

Nearly two months later China resumed adoptions. Soon after this we received our notification that we would be headed to China. What is amazing to think about is that if we had gone to China earlier, we would not have our Abby today. God knew what He was doing. Abby was never plan B; rather, she was God's plan for our family. She was never second, and she will always be first in our eyes.

That's the way God feels about the unqualified—we're always first in His eyes. You are not plan B. Rather, you are God's best chance at winning a lost and dying world! However, the next time you feel like plan B, just remember this prophecy about Jesus by the prophet Isaiah:

> He grew up before him like a tender shoot, and like a root out of dry ground. He had no beauty or majesty to attract us to him, nothing in his appearance that we should desire him. He was despised and rejected by mankind, a man of suffering, and familiar with pain. Like one from whom people hide their faces he was despised, and we held him in low esteem.
>
> —Isaiah 53:2–3

Does that sound like God's first choice? Yes, because Jesus did not come to seduce the eyes of man but to transform their hearts. That's how God intends to use you too.

Chapter 5

ROYALTY SOMETIMES COMES BROKEN

> "I've felt unqualified many times due to the brokenness of my past, but God chose to use my life for His glory and to bring healing to those who are brokenhearted."
>
> —Damian Martinez, Fort Lauderdale, FL

GOD IS RAISING up a generation of leaders who probably don't fit in, often look out of place, and really have no huge pedigree. It's what I call the company of the unqualified and unashamed. But the unqualified understand their qualification as a voice in God's kingdom does not come from human lineage.

In contrast, for years I've heard the line, "Those people are Christian royalty!" I first heard it in college when other students would point out someone with a great spiritual heritage or important last name. At first it can make you envious and wish you had a last name like theirs.

In those early years I would see people walk around like strutting peacocks, as if they had earned a right to be seen because of their family history. I was even jealous at times. That is, until I began to understand that there are no perfect families and that, most of all, we're called to establish our own legacy. My wife, Karen, made a great point when I shared this chapter with her. She said, "Does it really matter if people who are saved know your name when the lost have never heard of you?"

Of course, all of us should desire to have a good name. The Bible says, "A good name is more desirable than great riches; to be esteemed is better than silver or gold" (Prov. 22:1). My dad even used to say to me, "Son, protect our last name. Bring honor to it. You were born with nothing but a name, and it is with you until you die. Bring honor to our name."

I made up my mind early in life, then, to add value to our name, but to say I had a deep spiritual lineage like some of those other folks did would be far from the truth. In fact, being handed our last name was like being handed a clean slate because no one even knew our last name. If you said, "Schatzline," people would look at you as if you had just sneezed. After all, no one in our family had led a big ministry, pastored a large church, or conquered the distant lands of a mission field. Nope! No one was even saved until the middle of the 1970s. My parents were saved out of a life of drugs, crime, and pain. They started our lineage, and it continues today.

> "The unqualified are those who are overlooked and an afterthought, because they don't come from a rich spiritual heritage. They are those who are hidden in the shadows of the spiritual elite."
>
> —Mark McGaffin, youth pastor, Valencia, CA

You Can Lose Your Lineage

I believe the anointing can come into a home and grow with each generation—but it can also decrease. Many times I've seen people with a sense of entitlement squander away a lineage that was built before they existed. Isn't it true that each generation must choose how to represent the past? That's one of the reasons I decided to write this book—hoping that everyone reading it will understand that the unqualified are those who most likely don't come from a great history but are willing to establish a great future.

In terms of squandering away the past, I traveled to the northeast a couple years ago to do a television interview for my first book. I was excited about the interview because the television station had a rich heritage; a great leader who had established his ministry in the 1950s had started it.

Upon arriving at the television station, I went into an interview prep room, where I met the founder's grandson. I told him how honored I was to meet him, and he gave me a sigh and walked away. This seemed odd to me, but I chalked it up to it being very early in the day. I didn't realize at the time that this young leader didn't like some things I had written in my book.

Things gradually grew stranger as I sat on the couch for the interview. During the interview on camera, I was challenged on my social beliefs concerning homosexuality and whether or not a person can be born gay. I had written in my book that we are all born into a sin nature but that we are not born gay. I established my reason of thinking through research. I shared that I believe homosexuality is a by-product of an action, a choice, or an environment. The interviewer— who just so happened to be the grandson of the great leader I had met earlier—took a pretty belligerent tone with me. In truth, he was very angry at me. He said I was wrong in my convictions. He even accused me of hate speech.

I've often said that very soon the only "sin" recognized in certain churches will be bigotry toward ungodliness. In our day it is considered worse to judge evil than to do evil. But I stood my ground biblically with my beliefs, and after a fifteen-minute interview I was shown the door.

As I pulled away and headed back to the airport, I was overwhelmed with grief. I actually pulled off the road into a gas station to get my bearings. While flying home that day, I thought to myself, "It is not a lineage that makes you great but rather what you do each day that defines your own lineage." I also realized after that interview that we are losing the war of culture. The culture is doing everything it possibly can to reduce God down to an icon rather than a Savior. I found out later that the grandson was fired from the television network.

A Shepherd Called to a Palace

There are many greats in the Bible whom God raised up with no lineage, but there are two who truly represent what it means to be chosen by God and considered by everyone as unqualified. I have already mentioned one of them, Simon Peter, but the second is King David.

> "The unqualified is often the discounted of man but is counted on by God, not because of what he can do, but what God can do through him! He is the unexpected champion over the enemy of the throne, the shepherd-boy victor standing over the career-confident warrior! He is the secret weapon in the hand of God!"
>
> —Allen Hawes, youth pastor, The River, Tampa, FL

The life of King David is absolutely intriguing to me. He was someone no one saw coming on the scene—like pretty much every unqualified person God uses. David's story is a marvelous one when you realize he really was the last person who should have been chosen by God. God chose to raise him up in a time when the nation of Israel was living under the monarchy of a tortured soul by the name of King

Saul. He was a forgotten shepherd who rose to stardom with a sling and a harp.

David was ostracized from his family because, most likely, he was a product of his father's sexual mistakes. The Jewish oral tradition teaches that Jesse, David's father, had a relationship with a woman by the name of Nitzevet.[1] This caused David's family to hate and despise him. David would later write about his early years in Psalm 69: "For I endure scorn for your sake, and shame covers my face. I am a foreigner to my own family, a stranger to my own mother's children; for zeal for your house consumes me, and the insults of those who insult you fall on me" (vv. 7–9). His brothers didn't like him, and they did everything they could to ignore him. David was sent to work in the fields, where he would be isolated and forgotten.

> "It is the unqualified that must rise up from the ashes of past mistakes to step into the destiny that God has for them."
> —Phillip Hughes, 18, ministry student, Richmond, VA

Then everything changed. God called Samuel to anoint a new king in the house of Jesse, though Jesse didn't even invite David to the anointing. After Samuel tried to anoint each of the brothers but the oil didn't flow for any of them, he finally asked, "Is there not another?" God had already told Samuel that looks could be deceiving:

> When they arrived, Samuel took one look at Eliab and thought, "Here he is! GOD's anointed!"
> But GOD told Samuel, "Looks aren't everything. Don't be impressed with his looks and stature. I've already eliminated him. GOD judges persons

differently than humans do. Men and women look at the face; God looks into the heart."

—1 Samuel 16:6–7, The Message

They finally sent for David, and when he ran in from the fields, Samuel held the horn of oil over his head and the oil began to flow. We read that the Holy Spirit "entered David like a rush of wind, God vitally empowering him for the rest of his life" (1 Sam. 16:13, The Message).

"The unqualified is the selection process of identifying and eliminating people from consideration based on their lack of skill and imperfection. The assessment is based on experience, deep insight, and wisdom. In a moment's time a skilled leader can see, expose a multitude of faults, and quickly eliminate an unqualified from consideration. But then the Holy Spirit takes over. Years of experience fade, eyesight begins to dim, and conventional wisdom is thrown out the door. You see, when the Spirit is allowed into the process, the heart replaces conventional wisdom and the eyes no longer see the shepherd boy! We begin to see the king."

—Dan Holbrook, lead pastor, Wapakoneta, OH

Wow! God anointed an illegitimate kid to be the future king of Israel—a kid who was forgotten. This kid, armed only with a sling and a harp, was anointed to lead a nation.

I don't know about you, but that fires me up! In one day and in one moment a shepherd was anointed as king. Furthermore, he was anointed right in front of the ones who had looked down on him and despised his very existence.

If David had spent his life being groomed to lead the kingdom of Israel, this story wouldn't be nearly as special.

I imagine that his being anointed king absolutely shocked everyone. Remember, God doesn't look at polls or opinions when He chooses His leaders. He always looks for someone with a heart, regardless of what the world thinks. David was the least qualified to lead—his brothers were much more fit for it—yet God still used this nobody.

> "The unqualified ones are the Davids of this generation. They see victory when others see defeat. They are the ones who run with courage when others run with fear. They are God heroes in disguise. God causes the unqualified to succeed when people expect them to fail."
>
> —Micah Marshall, youth pastor, Altoona, PA

David had a long road ahead of him, though, before he actually took the throne. Even so, God saw fit to establish His plan in the midst of a pasture.

> Then he chose David, his servant, handpicked him from his work in the sheep pens. One day he was caring for the ewes and their lambs, the next day God had him shepherding Jacob, his people Israel, his prize possession. His good heart made him a good shepherd; he guided the people wisely and well.
> —PSALM 78:70–72, THE MESSAGE

You know what's crazy? That very day he was anointed, David went right back to doing what he was doing. Someone else in his place might have thought it was time to put on a robe and a crown, but not David. No, he understood that the *calling* of God without the *timing* of God would result in the *absence* of God.

In other words, keep doing what you're called to do until God makes the path known. David killed a giant, moved into the palace, and lived as a fugitive running from King Saul for many years. Finally, after his life as an exiled leader he was restored when King Saul and his three sons died in battle.

A Magnanimous King

Despite the fact that Saul had sought David's life again and again, David was heartbroken about the deaths of King Saul and his three sons because he loved Saul and Saul's family. He didn't throw a party over the death of his archenemy. The Bible says, in fact, "In lament, David ripped his clothes to ribbons. All the men with him did the same. They wept and fasted the rest of the day, grieving the death of Saul and his son Jonathan, and also the army of GOD and the nation Israel, victims in a failed battle" (2 Sam. 1:11–12, THE MESSAGE). David honored the anointing on Saul's life. It didn't matter that Saul had tried to harm David over and over. David looked past his personal pain and saw the touch of God upon Saul.

> "The unqualified have been brought out of brokenness, which attempted to define them, and instead are defined by the truth of their Savior."
>
> —Lauren Jenkins, 23,
> ministry student, Murfreesboro, TN

This generation of unqualified can learn from this that God is our defender. Never take matters into your own hands, because if you do, God will be forced to step back. The Bible is emphatic about this, especially when it comes to the anointing. Psalm 105:15 says, "Do not touch my anointed ones, and do no harm to my prophets" (MEV). In fact, when the servant who had helped Saul fall on his own sword informed David of Saul's death, it cost the servant his life because he had touched the anointed of the Lord (2 Sam. 1:14–15).

David honored Saul and never allowed bitterness to ruin his future. It is for this reason that David was used so mightily as a king who restored justice and hope.

> "The unqualified are those whose brokenness and broken hearts have been mended by the broken body of our Savior. The weaknesses and cracks in our earthen-vessel lives only serve as windows for His glory and strength to shine through."
>
> —Doug Witherup, district youth director and author, Concord, NC

David never forgot it was Saul who had given him his first position as a worship leader in the royal court of the king. First Samuel 16:17–19 (THE MESSAGE) tells us:

> Saul told his servants, "Go ahead. Find me someone who can play well and bring him to me." One of the young men spoke up, "I know someone. I've seen him myself: the son of Jesse of Bethlehem, an excellent musician. He's also courageous, of age, well-spoken, and good-looking. And GOD is with him." So Saul sent messengers to Jesse requesting, "Send your son David to me, the one who tends the sheep."

David had worked for this mad king. He knew how angry Saul could get and the demons that tormented him. Yet David stayed faithful to the call of God. I believe David was probably just honored to be desired by someone, even though he would eventually have to flee for his own safety.

A Humility of Heart

What I love about David is that he knew where he came from. He never forgot those lonely days in the pasture when no one knew his name, the days when he was despised and he found deep solace through worship and hunting. Now he was a king, and he understood that the position is never more powerful than the blessing. After all, David was an unqualified nobody. He probably spent his days wondering how in the world he got his job!

> "The unqualified is an abused and suicidal seventeen-year-old girl who was kicked out of her home for accepting Christ and years later is called by God to bring down spiritual strongholds that have been holding a generation back from knowing the hope that only Christ can bring."
>
> —Theresa "Mama T" Lance,
> intercessor, Fort Wayne, IN

When David finally became king, he set about to establish his rule, and one of the first things he did was ask a very powerful question: "Is there anyone still left of the house of Saul to whom I can show kindness for Jonathan's sake?" (2 Sam. 9:1). This question may seem strange to you and me. After all, David had finally rid himself of the very man who had chased him all over the country and tried to destroy him for the last two decades.

It *is* strange—unless you understand that David loved Saul and his family. Saul's son Jonathan was David's best friend. Jonathan even protected David when Saul tried to kill him. Their friendship was very strong, and on one occasion David and Jonathan had a deep conversation that ended with a covenant promise. Jonathan said, "Go in peace! The two of us have vowed friendship in GOD's name, saying, 'GOD will be the bond between me and you, and between my children and your children forever!'" (1 Sam. 20:42, THE MESSAGE). Jonathan was now dead, but a covenant outlasts the grave. So David asked if there was anyone he could bless because of his friend Jonathan.

One thing drives the truly called of God: the sound of the hurting, weary, wounded, and sorrowful that pushes us past our limits. If someone says they are called but doesn't hear the voices of the hurting, then I challenge their calling. In fact, I say maybe they're not really called, but rather are being seduced by the stage. Amazingly that is exactly what King David represented. He was just a man who had tripped over his destiny, despite the fact that he was a shepherd at heart.

"Is there anyone left?" David asked. To say this, David had to be a big person. He knew any survivor from the house of Saul would naturally have been the rightful heir to the throne of Israel. Yet David was adamant about keeping a promise he had made to a dead prince. This is because when you really get blessed, you're never stingy. Blessed people are givers because they know they shouldn't even be where they are. They know that if it were not for the grace of God, they would still be back where they started.

The Day a Prince Lost a Kingdom

Ziba told the king, "Yes, there is Jonathan's son, lame in both feet."

"Where is he?"

"He's living at the home of Makir son of Ammiel in Lo Debar."

King David didn't lose a minute. He sent and got him from the home of Makir son of Ammiel in Lo Debar.

—2 Samuel 9:3–5, The Message

Now let me take you back to a day when someone else in the story—a would-be prince—lost everything. In fact, this would-be prince didn't just lose the palace, he also lost his family. He didn't just lose his king, he also lost his dad. He didn't just lose his standing in line for the throne, he also lost his ability to stand.

In 2 Samuel 4 we hear how this would-be prince lost his footing:

> It so happened that Saul's son, Jonathan, had a son who was maimed in both feet. When he was five years old, the report on Saul and Jonathan came from Jezreel. His nurse picked him up and ran, but in her hurry to get away she fell, and the boy was maimed. His name was Mephibosheth.
>
> —2 SAMUEL 4:4, THE MESSAGE

Can you see this story as it unfolds? Word of the deaths of the king and the prince reach the palace, and everyone panics in fear for their lives. Mephibosheth's caretaker, in order to save herself, forgets about the boy lying in her lap. When she jumps to her feet, she drops him. Now in the worst moment of this young boy's life, he would find himself crashing to the floor after being dropped by the one who was in charge of his safety.

This future king was supposed to have grown strong and lead, but now he was crippled. We know Saul was a tall and strong man according to scripture, but now Saul's grandson was a cripple. Never to run! Never to jump! And never to stand strong in front of the army he was called to someday lead. He was royalty, and in one moment his life was over. His very name, Mephibosheth, in Hebrew means the "exterminator of shame"![2] This boy was to be a great leader. He was to be a restorer of hope. His very name carried greatness, but now greatness lay broken on the floor. He was now unqualified.

Have you ever been dropped? Maybe it was in the early years that the divorce or the death happened. It wasn't supposed to happen that way, and now you don't run as fast as you used to. One moment affects all other moments.

I have never met anyone who has been greatly used by

God who didn't also have a limp. What do I mean? The storms and hurts of life make us most effective. How you survive the senseless seasons determines your ability to lead others. My wife, Karen, always says, "It is impossible to have compassion without first having pain." What you have been through is what God will use to heal others.

> "The unqualified is the felon, the divorced single mother, the broken soul who sees no hope. I am eternally grateful that God qualifies the unqualified! What the devil tried to destroy me with, God has used to build my destiny!"
>
> —Nicole Sawyer Richey, worship leader, Decatur, AL

All through the Bible we see future great leaders who were dropped at a young age. Moses was dropped in a river. Joseph was dropped in a pit. And Jesus was dropped to the earth to become humanity's sacrificial Lamb. We have all been dropped, but God has called us to get back up. He can use us if we're willing to stand again.

A Broken Prince Without a Voice

Have you ever been through something so terrible that you can't even talk about it? The Bible says Mephibosheth was forced to go and live in a place called Lo Debar. The name Lo Debar means "no pasture"[3] or "no communication."[4] He lived in a place of no rest and no communication, in other words.

The enemy's goal is to harm you so badly that you can't talk about it. He wants to silence lambs through intimidation, frustration, trials, and tribulation.

Here was the would-be prince living in a place where he couldn't talk about his pain. He had no idea a king would come calling for him. Restoration was on the way. God always remembers His covenant. In the case of Mephibosheth, it was a covenant between two friends from long ago.

Finally, the day came when Mephibosheth went to the palace. A knock came on the door; the would-be prince had arrived. The servants scurried here and there, putting everything in place. King David was about to meet the man who had a rightful place on his throne.

I can see David as he walks to the door. Can you? I imagine he opened the door slowly so as to not show too much excitement. There in front of him stood the servant Ziba, and in his arms was a broken, weary, wounded, and dirty man with legs turned inward. He was no longer the "exterminator of shame" but rather the representative of pain. David was ready to greet one who should have been a mighty warrior, but instead, there in front of him was someone who had been dropped.

Do you know what it's like for someone to look at you and expect you to be one thing and find out you're really something else? You're not what they thought you would be. We don't want people to know who we really are! We are so good at wearing our masks to cover our pain, but sooner or later our true identity is exposed. How will we respond once it is?

> "My whole life, I have been deemed unqualified. I've grown up with a speech impediment, but God has called me to become an evangelist. God ignored my limitations and is using me for other people's freedom."
>
> —David Ferguson, ministry student and future evangelist, Cedar Hill, TX

What makes this story so profound is that David was uniquely qualified to help this unqualified, broken man. David knew what it was like to be dropped by the ones who were supposed to take care of him too. He had compassion for Mephibosheth because Mephibosheth's father had compassion on David.

> "Don't be afraid," David said to him, "for I will surely show you kindness for the sake of your father Jonathan. I will restore to you all the land that belonged to your grandfather Saul, and you will always eat at my table."
>
> Mephibosheth bowed down and said, "What is your servant, that you should notice a dead dog like me?"
>
> Then the king summoned Ziba, Saul's steward, and said to him, "I have given your master's grandson everything that belonged to Saul and his family. You and your sons and your servants are to farm the land for him and bring in the crops, so that your master's grandson may be provided for. And Mephibosheth, grandson of your master, will always eat at my table." (Now Ziba had fifteen sons and twenty servants.)
>
> —2 SAMUEL 9:7–10

One of my favorite parts of this story is when Mephibosheth calls himself a dead dog. Did you notice the king never responded? In most kingdoms of that day a newly crowned king would kill all the family of the previous king in order to secure his throne. Instead, David told the servant that everything had been restored to the broken prince. The Bible says from that day forward Mephibosheth would eat at the king's table. He would be considered a part of the family!

I can imagine Mephibosheth felt out of place as he sat down to eat with the king's family. After all, he was unqualified to be there at the king's table—that is, until the king made a royal decree that his table belonged to the unqualified cripple.

This is exactly what Jesus does for you and me. We're seated at the table of the King! He accepts us and restores what has been robbed from us, and our royalty is restored.

> And He raised us up and seated us together in the
> heavenly places in Christ Jesus.
>
> —EPHESIANS 2:6, MEV

> But you are a chosen race, a royal priesthood, a holy
> nation, a people for God's own possession, so that you
> may declare the goodness of Him who has called you
> out of darkness into His marvelous light.
>
> —1 PETER 2:9, MEV

Walk with me now into the king's dining room. The servants are again running to and fro. Music plays in the background. You can almost hear that song from Disney's *Beauty and the Beast*, "Be Our Guest." The room is beautifully adorned with the finest tapestry, china, table, chairs, and pictures that large sums of money can buy.

As King David walks in from a side door, the entire family stands to greet him—that is, all except Mephibosheth, who cannot stand and therefore remains in his seat. As the family sits down for supper, I can see the king's kids—Absalom, Amnon, and Tamar—laughing about the events of the day.

Then King David looks down the table and says, "Mephibosheth, tell me about your day!"

The crippled prince looks up, clears his throat, and says, "Your majesty, um, it has been a long time since anyone asked me about my day."

"Well, welcome home! Your day matters to us!"

With tears streaming down his face, perhaps Mephibosheth says, "Today was glorious! I visited the room where I was dropped as a small boy, and I shouted as loud as I could, 'Devil, you didn't win!'"

The room erupts in applause. Can you just see it?

Someday you too will shout in the room where you should have died. You will praise at the place that tried to quiet you. For now just enjoy being a part of the family of God.

How blessed is God! And what a blessing he is! He's
the Father of our Master, Jesus Christ, and takes us to
the high places of blessing in him. Long before he laid
down earth's foundations, he had us in mind, had set-
tled on us as the focus of his love, to be made whole
and holy by his love. Long, long ago he decided to
adopt us into his family through Jesus Christ. (What
pleasure he took in planning this!) He wanted us to
enter into the celebration of his lavish gift-giving by
the hand of his beloved Son.

—EPHESIANS 1:3–6, THE MESSAGE

A final banquet is coming, and you and I are invited. I'm
pretty sure my place at the table and yours will have a card
that reads, "The Unqualified Remnant of God." Don't you
want to be there to receive it?

> "The unqualified are often the discounted of man, but
> counted on by God—not because of what they can do,
> but what God can do through them! The unqualified
> are the unexpected champions over the enemy of the
> throne—like the shepherd boy victor standing over
> the career, confident warrior! The unqualified are the
> secret weapon in the hand of God!"
>
> —Allen Hawes, youth pastor, The River, Tampa, FL

SECTION II

THE UNQUALIFIED MUST EXPERIENCE . . .

Chapter 6

THE SEPARATION

"It is the unqualified that were once bound by situations, problems, and failures but now dance over them without dignity because God has equipped them with freedom."

—Jerrica Artis, 23, Richmond, VA

I N THIS CHAPTER I will confront the biggest battle that keeps the unqualified from ever stepping into their destiny. It's the battle of separation from the world.

Remember, Jesus never called you to fit in and be a part of this world. We've already covered that. But the battle to break free from the world is very intense, and the force to be a part of this world is one that is only conquered by dying to your flesh. The drawing force of the world can stop the unqualified in their tracks. This force is the reason there are those who we've never heard of but should have. It's also strong enough to cause those with great reputations in the kingdom of God to falter.

There's a real danger here of stepping into the gray area of trying to live in both worlds. But there is no gray area. The war is real! Jesus said, "This is war, and there is no neutral ground. If you're not on my side, you're the enemy; if you're not helping, you're making things worse" (Matt. 12:30, THE MESSAGE).

We were born into a world that's becoming darker and

more sinister each day. God knew it was going to get worse, and He decided the time for you to be here on the earth is now. He trusts that you will make a stand. He's been watching you since the beginning.

> Like an open book, you watched me grow from conception to birth; all the stages of my life were spread out before you, the days of my life all prepared before I'd even lived one day.
> —PSALM 139:16, THE MESSAGE

So God has massive plans for us, but so does Satan. This is your moment! Will you rise to the occasion, walk past your fears, and lead a Holy Spirit revolution for God? The plan of God requires a response.

The Outbreak

So here's the situation we're facing. Imagine yourself sitting down in front of the TV to relax after a long day, when suddenly a breaking news flash breaks into your program. "Breaking news!" the news anchor says. "There's been an outbreak of disease in unprecedented proportion."

> "The unqualified are those that have felt unworthy, that once settled for a life of 'less than' because of the shame and guilt from their past, but now freely, passionately, in total surrender pursue the high calling they have in Christ Jesus. The unqualified have overcome their biggest hurdle: the hurdle of ME!"
> —Keith Daugherty, pastor, New Jersey

You run to the window of your home just in time to see mass hysteria breaking out in the streets. Sirens begin to sound all over your city. You hear the noise of a helicopter somewhere above your home. A loudspeaker from the helicopter announces, "Your city has been quarantined. Everyone must stay inside until a cure is found!"

Of course, this has really happened. The disease I am speaking of here is called sin.

With sin came the invasion of other attributes into our world, including sickness, fear, death, perversion, anger, and deception. The disease called sin went viral in a garden nearly seven thousand years ago. That is where the carrier of the disease made an uninvited guest appearance into God's created utopia. The disease interrupted God's plan for humanity. The carrier disguised himself as a conniving snake that would seduce humanity into relinquishing their God-given authority. He hasn't stopped working his will for thousands of years. In fact, he grows into a full-blown dragon by the time we reach the Book of Revelation!

> "The unqualified is someone who has no spiritual upbringing or background and has tried everything the world has to offer yet still feels empty and useless inside. Then God plants a seed of 'There is something more.' They are the ones with contrite and willing hearts, callouses on their knees, and only desire to hear from the King, 'Well done, good and faithful servant.'"
>
> —Roger Shadley, business owner and lay minister, Phoenix, AZ

How is this possible?

It is very simple. We know God cursed the serpent to eat of the dust in Genesis 3. Dust? Yep, dust! What are you and I made of? We are made of dust too, and our flesh will eventually become dust. Satan literally feeds off our flesh. We must not live according to our flesh, then, but the Spirit! A separation must take place.

Unfortunately, though, we're living in a time when it's hard to know where people stand on issues. There's been a graying of the lines between the righteous and the unrighteous. If we don't understand the difference, people will never get free. We'll just keep sanctifying demons and delegating our God-given authority to the propagators of political correctness. The greatest way to inoculate the world from the message of the gospel is to water the gospel down to simply "good ideas" and "overzealous speech."

But here's the truth. The enemy is trying to take you out. There has been a plan to limit you and quiet you since the day you were born. The apostle Peter said it best: "Dear friends, do not be surprised at the fiery ordeal that has come on you to test you, as though something strange were happening to you" (1 Pet. 4:12). He went on to say in verse 13 that we should even rejoice in the sufferings of Christ. That is most definitely easier said than done. We are called to be overcomers, but this is very hard when we are living in a day where we seem to be overrun!

The Devil Is Real

The Bible speaks clearly about who Satan is and his plan of destruction for each of us. John 10:10 gives us his job description: "The thief comes only to steal and kill and destroy; I have come that they may have life, and have it to the full." Furthermore, the enemy is on the prowl. My friend pastor Mark Spitsbergen said to me recently, "The devil prowls around like a roaring lion looking for someone to devour, but God goes about as the lion seeking whom He may empower!"

A sleeping church and lethargic Christians will never send demons scurrying for cover. The devil understands this. That is why he's so methodical in his attacks on you and me. We must awaken to his attacks! He knows if he can continue to defeat the believer with fear, discouragement, and hurt, that particular believer will never rise up and lead against his agenda.

Let me be very clear here—we have seen nothing yet. There is coming a day when Satan will stand unabated and make a mockery of anything and everything Christian. After all, he is the god of this age! The apostle Paul said, "The god of this age has blinded the minds of unbelievers, so that they cannot see the light of the gospel that displays the glory of Christ, who is the image of God" (2 Cor. 4:4).

God has called you to see Him in clarity. You must stay in pursuit! Dive into God's Word and let it be your road map.

> How can a young person live a clean life? By carefully reading the map of your Word. I'm single-minded in pursuit of you; don't let me miss the road signs you've posted. I've banked your promises in the vault of my heart so I won't sin myself bankrupt. Be blessed, GOD; train me in your ways of wise living. I'll transfer to my lips all the counsel that comes from your mouth; I delight far more in what you tell me about living than in gathering a pile of riches. I ponder every morsel of wisdom from you, I attentively watch how you've done it. I relish everything you've told me of life, I won't forget a word of it.
> —PSALM 119:9–16, THE MESSAGE

When you realize that without God you would be absolutely doomed, it changes your perspective on your own abilities. Remember, we are the unqualified! That means we couldn't possibly win without the help of our Savior Jesus. Remember our key verse for this entire book:

> For observe your calling, brothers. Among you, not many wise men according to the flesh, not many mighty men, and not many noble men were called. But God has chosen the foolish things of the world to confound the wise. God has chosen the weak things

> of the world to confound the things which are mighty.
> And God has chosen the base things of the world and
> things which are despised. Yes, and He chose things
> which did not exist to bring to nothing things that do.
> —1 CORINTHIANS 1:26–28, MEV

If you go on to read verse 29 it says, "That no flesh should boast in His presence" (MEV). Our flesh has to die in the presence of God, because Jesus became flesh for us. He took back our lives on the cross (Rom. 8:3).

The only way we will bring our nation back from the brink—the only way we will see God's glory restored on the earth—is to reverse the curse. We must confront the contagion called sin. Why do I call it contagion? Because *contagion* means the following: "harmful or undesirable contact or influence; the ready transmission or spread as of an idea or emotion from person to person."[1] Sin has but one goal: to separate us from our Creator.

Breaking the Yokes

> Do not be unequally yoked together with unbelievers.
> For what fellowship has righteousness with unrigh-
> teousness? What communion has light with darkness?
> —2 CORINTHIANS 6:14, MEV

I've heard thousands of stories from Christians who just couldn't break free from the yoke of the enemy. This has forced me to come to the conclusion that we will never win a lost and dying world until those who are called to heal others are first healed themselves.

What is a yoke? It's "a wooden beam normally used between a pair of oxen or other animals to enable them to pull together on a load when working in pairs, as oxen usually do; some yokes are fitted to individual animals."[2] The lesson of the yoke is that what we are tied to determines the direction of our lives. When we become yoked with the wrong people or things, we go the wrong direction.

I have never met a believer who did not first have to get free from old yokes of bondage. Maybe it is freedom from old relationships, a broken heart, addictions, or the lies of false identity. We all have to get free. A yoke has the ability to keep you from realizing how powerful you are in Christ.

I have met so many young believers in Christ who struggle with the old life because they refuse to break ties with the old. That is why the apostle Paul went on to say, "For what do righteousness and wickedness have in common?" (2 Cor. 6:14).

I believe we are called to minister to the lost, but God has never called us to be tied to them. When two animals are yoked together, the strongest animal always takes the lead. It is so easy to be led by what you haven't conquered. So the scripture declares that you have to break away. When you give everything to God, that means what used to own you now has no claim on your life. Jesus purchased you, and now He wants to lead you into covenant with Him. That means you have to separate from the things, people, and bondages that have held you back.

Today, in many instances, the church is teaching that in order to win the world, we have to be like the world. That is a lie. I often hear the argument that Jesus loved the sinner and despised the religious—that He even dined with the sinners. That is absolutely true, but Jesus never became like the sinner. Instead, He was so strong in His belief system that He was able to effect change in others without being infected Himself. We are all called to impact our Jerusalem, but we must remember that doesn't mean we become like what we are called to win. Remember, Jesus was crucified in Jerusalem!

Think of the way elephants are trained. This can be a helpful word picture. When elephants are very small, they have a rope tied around one foot. The rope is then tied to a stake in the ground. As a small elephant, they are too small to break free, and as they get older, they become strong enough to break free but don't realize they can. Their minds are conditioned to believe the tiny stake in the ground is stronger than them, a three-ton beast. They are yoked to something much smaller than them, but their minds don't believe they can break free. They are so conditioned to believe that freedom is out of the question and bondage is a way of life that they never even try to break free.

Jesus came to set us free from the stake in the ground. That is why the cross was stuck in the ground, chaining up our sin and releasing us to victory. He breaks the bondage of sin: "It is for freedom that Christ has set us free. Stand firm, then, and do not let yourselves be burdened again by a yoke of slavery" (Gal. 5:1). You have to break free from what enslaves you. When you're still entangled and owned by the sin Christ died to release you from, aren't you really saying that the cross wasn't powerful enough to free you?

At the moment you gave your heart to God, He began a new work. Second Corinthians 5:17 declares, "Therefore, if any man is in Christ, he is a new creature. Old things have passed away. Look, all things have become new" (MEV). You must make up your mind that the freedom that came from the cross can not only save you but also keep you. At the moment you receive salvation, you declare that the light that shines in you is greater than the darkness trying to invade you.

How do you get free from the old ways? The Bible speaks of only one thing that breaks yokes, and that's the anointing. According to Isaiah 10:27, "In that day his burden shall be taken away from off your shoulder, and his yoke from off your neck; and the yoke shall be destroyed because of the anointing oil" (MEV). It is the power of God at work in our lives that brings the freedom. Dive into God's Word. Pray in the Spirit. Worship without limitation. Declare that God is bigger than your issue. Allow the anointing to begin to bring the separation your soul so desperately needs. Remember, God is not anti-fun, but He is anti-bondage! God gives us precepts and boundaries to guide us into a life of freedom.

> "It is the unqualified that will raise the standard of consecration and strive after the true meaning of holiness."
>
> —Hannah Mott, 19, ministry student, Columbus, GA

The Dating Game

For many years my wife and I were youth pastors. The 2 Corinthians 6:14 scripture about being unequally yoked was always our first response when dealing with students concerning what relationships they should pursue in their lives. Whether it was friendships or choosing a mate to date, this was always a major issue among singles, young and old. We always warned about being unequally yoked with the wrong person. Jeanne Mayo has always said, "Show me your friends, and I will show you your future!"

Now that I am older, I have seen the devastation of what wrong yokes can do to someone's future. I used to call this "missionary dating"—when someone who has chosen to live a life pursuing God decides to get involved with someone who doesn't have the same beliefs, convictions, or standards, thinking they can bring them into God's fold. In truth these believers are setting themselves up for failure. When you try to convince yourself that you have the power to change a person after you've decided to love them, heartbreak usually happens.

I have known so many who had the hand of God upon their lives but then chose to go outside the boundaries of

Christianity through unequal yoking in their dating lives, only to make decisions and choices that temporarily halted their destinies or destroyed where they could have been for God. I remember warning one very precious young lady in particular about a certain guy. This girl was deeply involved in our youth ministry, led a campus Bible club, and was sold out. Then this much older single guy began to pursue her. We warned her to run away from him, and I even warned the guy to leave her alone. We went so far as to talk to her parents, but they liked the guy and opened their home up to him. I knew his track record and warned the parents of his history. The parents actually told me to stay out of it and mind my own business. So I backed away and watched a trail of destruction take place. The girl eventually fell away, married the guy, and after several hard years of marriage was left broken and deserted.

Here's the truth. God has an incredible plan for your future that includes the person of your dreams. You must not settle for a cheap imitation or thrill that could cost you your future.

> Your spring water is for you and you only, not to be passed around among strangers. Bless your fresh-flowing fountain! Enjoy the wife you married as a young man! Lovely as an angel, beautiful as a rose—don't ever quit taking delight in her body. Never take her love for granted! Why would you trade enduring intimacies for cheap thrills with a whore? for dalliance with a promiscuous stranger?
> —PROVERBS 5:17–20, THE MESSAGE

Take Karen's and my story as an example. I will never forget the night I met this woman who was to be my future wife. There she stood, across the room in the middle of the youth sanctuary at Eagle Lake Assembly of God in Eagle Lake, Florida. She was absolutely stunning. I was just finishing my first year of college at Southeastern University. A friend of mine had asked me to go to the church service with him that night. I wish I could say we went for spiritual reasons, but the fact is that he wanted me to go to the service with him so he could check out a girl. He said, "Schatz"—that was my nickname in college—"there is this gorgeous girl at this church that I want to go to tonight. Why don't you go with me?" I said, "Sure, let's go!" Well, it turned out that the gorgeous girl he was speaking of was Karen Brown, the girl I would marry. In fact, when I saw Karen, I said to my friend, "Sorry, man. I am going to marry her."

That night I met Karen, and we talked for a moment, but the timing just wasn't right. It wasn't until several months later that I would see her again. In between the time I first saw Karen and the time I would see her again, God did a major work in my heart. God had asked me to focus on Him and not date anyone for a very long season. Actually it wasn't that long. It was only about six months.

Nevertheless, during that time of dating abstinence, I got my priorities right in many areas. God began to teach me about loving Him first above all else. When Karen and I finally met again and began to date, we both knew we were meant for each other. Karen was shy, and I was loud and crazy. She was not only beautiful and brilliant, but she also was very pure. I had never met anyone like her.

We later found out we had both written a letter to God describing the person we wanted to marry someday. Our lists matched each other's perfectly. We had both described to the Lord our hearts' desires. This included spiritual, intellectual, and of course physical.

Had I not taken six months off from dating and learned God's heart at a deeper level, I honestly believe I would have never met Karen.

We were married September 29, 1990. We were young, in love, and broke! Yet it was those early years that gave us a foundation. We learned to laugh, pray, and play together. We both had dreams, and we joined them together.

Karen always knew she was called into the ministry. Her mom used to tell her when she was a child that someday she would marry a preacher. What really happened, though, is that I married a powerful prophetic woman of God who has transformed tens of thousands of lives.

Who would have thought that the young, shy girl from Eagle Lake, Florida, would end up traveling the world, transforming lives, raising two amazing kids, and becoming a signed author for a major publisher? The answer is Jesus and I did.

I must admit that in our early years, I thought that because I was raised in ministry and Karen was not that somehow I was superior in the kingdom and that I would show her the ropes. I was dead wrong. One day in prayer God spoke to me about this. He said, "Pat, the reason you have been so blessed is because you also walk in the anointing that I have placed upon Karen. The two of you are one. You are to honor her ministry above yours at all times." I remember going to Karen and repenting for not truly understanding what God had given me.

God has a plan for you and me. We are not called to settle for seconds. We live in a time where if something doesn't work, we want a do over. We must trust that when God brings two people together, He has a plan. Trust Him! Guard your heart and wait on the person God has prepared for you.

I'll take this one step further and challenge you to be so very careful of yokes not just in choosing a mate, but also in business and ministry partnerships. The question you should always be willing to ask is, "Can this person make the light of God in me dim or glow brighter?" Listen to the Holy Spirit, and He will give you the answer. It is the agreement test: "Can two people walk together without agreeing on the direction?" (Amos 3:3, NLT). When there is a supernatural God agreement, then the miraculous can happen (Matt. 18:19). But if you can't walk with someone in agreement, then you're wasting your time.

> "The unqualified cannot hope to achieve notoriety or any lasting legacy without the ability to overcome the lie that their qualification must be based on education, wealth, or status. In my city there has been only one means to destroy that lie: an authentic encounter with the fire of God!"
>
> —Forrest Beiser, pastor, San Francisco, CA

The Separation of Righteousness

In 2 Corinthians 6:14 Paul asks, "For what do righteousness and wickedness have in common?" He is not asking a question so much as declaring the two are totally different. To choose righteousness means that you strive to walk out your God-given destiny separate from the world. You are choosing to walk a straight path that lines up with God's character. This means you are not bending or flowing with the world's desires. You admit no gray areas. You choose a life of consecration.

Often we become so immersed in the world in which we live that we lose our ability to tell right from wrong. God has called you to be different. I have often heard it said, "If you don't stand for something, you will fall for anything." Until you make up your mind that God's Word doesn't change and His character is our compass, you will continually struggle with the war of two kingdoms. But I have never met anyone who regretted choosing to ignore the lies of culture in order to pursue righteousness. That means when the

Holy Spirit quickens you inside with a "gut check," you have to run from evil.

Righteousness is not an arrogant act but rather a broken and humble response to the love of God. Righteousness means agreeing with God! I choose righteousness not because of the law of God but because of the holiness of a Savior. My choosing to live a life of righteousness is a direct reflection of being rescued by God. If it costs me friendship, promotion, or even accolades then I say, "Good-bye to what could never keep me!"

The reflection in the mirror should be that of Jesus's humility, not the costume of compromise. But the world will never understand righteousness because it has never encountered God on His terms. James said, "Draw near to God, and He will draw near to you. Cleanse your hands, you sinners, and purify your hearts, you double-minded" (James 4:8, MEV). When a person doesn't walk in righteousness, it is proof they're still camping at the tree of the knowledge of good and evil. This means they are eating the fruit of death, which Christ came to redeem. The unqualified know this and have taken Christ up on His offer and live a set-apart life of gratitude from then on.

The Light of Separation

What communion has light with darkness?
—2 CORINTHIANS 6:14, MEV

When darkness exists in our lives that means we have not allowed God full access. Turn on the light! God is light, and in Him there is no darkness (1 John 1:5).

Satan will always do everything he can to keep you in the dark. I have often heard people say when talking about sin in their lives, "I just don't feel convicted about that." I have to always ask in response, "Have you invited God to turn on the light?" We need the light! I have found in my darkest moments that if I will turn the light of God on in my life, I will find treasures.

> And I will give you the treasures of darkness and hidden riches of secret places so that you may know that I, the LORD, who calls you by your name, am the God of Israel.
>
> —ISAIAH 45:3, MEV

We must realize that God will always rescue us no matter what situation we are in. Every time we have messed up and wandered away from God, we know that He has seen it. All we have to do is call out to Him and He will rescue us. When God comes in, the darkness has to flee! Jesus said, "I have come as a light into the world, that whoever believes in Me should not remain in darkness" (John 12:46, MEV). Jesus also gave us this powerful promise:

> For a brief time still, the light is among you. Walk by the light you have so darkness doesn't destroy you. If you walk in darkness, you don't know where you're going. As you have the light, believe in the light. Then the light will be within you, and shining through your lives. You'll be children of light.
>
> —JOHN 12:35–36, THE MESSAGE

Turn the light on before we run out of time. There is darkness all around us. We are the lighthouses to rescue the hurting!

> "The unqualified are overlooked by the general populace but are chosen by God before the foundation of the world."
>
> —India Carter, 21, ministry student, Columbus, GA

The Separation From Belial

> What agreement has Christ with Belial? Or what part
> has he who believes with an unbeliever?
> —2 CORINTHIANS 6:15, MEV

What in the world is Belial? That sounds like some mystical creature in a movie or video game rated M for maturity. (Believe it or not, Belial is actually a name used in video games, and it is also the title of a video game!)

Belial is a very real entity. The apostle Paul uses this name because it is another name for Satan or lawlessness. I believe that when the apostle Paul spoke of Belial, he was declaring the very personality of Satan. In fact, the word *Belial* is used throughout the Bible to describe those who made war with God.

This word was used in the description of the sons of Eli the High Priest in 1 Samuel 2:12: "Now the sons of Eli were sons of Belial; they knew not the LORD" (KJV). That scripture is speaking of Hophni and Phinehas. These two boys were evil scoundrels. They had no regard for the things of God. They had sex with the women in the temple and even stole the sacrifices made to God. That is why Eli's house fell into judgment and God raised up Samuel to transform the house of God. That is also why they were called the sons of Belial.

Did you know that Belial is not only the name of Satan, but also a pronoun that means "worthless"[3] and "never to rise"? That's right, the very definition of Belial contains the characteristics infecting a generation. "Worthlessness" and "never to rise" could be the label sewn onto the lives of many. The devil wants to stop you from realizing that God has massive plans for you, so he tries to inflict you with the two characteristics he embodies.

These two characteristics work hand in hand. In fact, statistics say that more than 5 percent of both men and women in the United States experience the horrible feeling of worthlessness,[4] and the statistic is so much higher for those who are called. The Schaeffer Institute cited the astounding statistic that 70 percent of pastors battle with depression.[5] How could this be? These are the messengers of God! It is simple. I believe the attack is so much greater on the called because if they are not free, then the enemy quiets the voice God has called to bring freedom.

> "The unqualified are the ones who kill their flesh daily, because they know the impossible is only possible through Jesus."
>
> —Aarynton Smith, 19,
> ministry student, Terre Haute, IN

Worthlessness is the dirtiest of all demonic forces. It has caused a generation to hate themselves, self-mutilate, and even take their own lives. It will keep you from never rising above your own self-deception. If the devil can make you feel worthless, then you will never know the power of loving others, because the way you feel about yourself will determine how you treat others.

Many times we allow the opinion of others to define what we are or will become. Maybe you were told that you were dumb, ugly, or illegitimate and those words froze your life in a prison of self-depreciation. Worthlessness has the ability to force a person to climb into a hole and never want to come out. If worthlessness takes over, then eventually you become a POW-MIA—powerless offended warrior who is missing in action!

Breaking Free to Dance

I must admit that I spent many years having to confront worthlessness in my own life. Finally, one day I decided enough was enough and I cried out to God. The date was August 21, 2012, and the words that I heard from God were piercing. He said, "Pat, are you willing to dance where you could die?"

I was ministering in Littlestown, Pennsylvania, at the church of a dear friend named Jim Ruddy. My hotel was a few miles away in the town of Gettysburg. I love visiting that part of the nation because it is so rich in history.

I had awakened that morning with a deep stirring that I must pray. As I was readying myself to go for a morning jog and pray, I decided to jog the rolling hills of the Gettysburg battlefield. This was the site of the greatest battle in American history that took place during the Civil War on July 1–3, 1863. During those three days between 43,000 and 51,000 soldiers from both armies were casualties in the three-day battle.[6] Today it is a major tourist attraction, but once you begin to walk the battlefield it is very quieting and sobering. This battlefield represents the will of man to overcome bigotry and slavery.

Early that morning I had felt an overwhelming spirit of failure upon me. For years I have fought this spirit. In fact, I thought I had defeated this spirit by, well, willing it away. Meaning, I would say to myself, "Come on, Pat, keep going! Don't let it win! You're an overcomer! You're a man chosen by God!" It was the same spirit I had faced more than twenty-five years before at the youth pastors' conference I mentioned earlier.

As I jogged through the Gettysburg battlefield that morning, I began to worship past my private pain that I had hidden so long with my public persona. Then I heard the Lord say these words: "When will I be enough for you?"

I said, "Lord, You are more than enough!"

Then He said something that challenged everything in me. He said, "Pat, are you willing to dance where you could die?"

Now, the Gettysburg battlefield represents the place of

death. So my response to God was simple. I said, "Lord, that is crazy! Are You asking me to dance before You right here?"

I couldn't believe that God was asking me to dance in public—and not just any public place, but a national park with tourists riding buses, families on vacation, and the optics of park rangers.

God spoke to me again. "Pat, are you willing to dance where you could die?"

I said, "Yes, Lord, I will praise You!"

As I began to praise, the presence of God overwhelmed me in such a powerful and profound way. I began to weep and dance. I am sure the tourists thought to themselves, "Who is that crazy guy dancing?" But I have learned there are times where your freedom is dependent on whether you're willing to die to the flesh to live in the Spirit.

After probably thirty minutes of worship I decided I needed to call my wife and tell her what God was doing in me. I felt such a boldness and freedom in my spirit. I called her via FaceTime so we could see each other face-to-face. With red eyes and a tear-stained face I made the call. When Karen answered, I explained to her what God had spoken to me to do. I shared with her that a new freedom had come over me and that I realized it was time for major changes in our life.

I suddenly understood the love of God like I had never before in my forty-two years on earth. During our call Karen wept with me as I repented for three things. I said, "Karen, for years you have never known who you would wake up next to in the morning. Would it be an on-fire evangelist ready to change the world? Would it be a loving husband and dad who simply wanted time with his family? Or would it be a defeated, weary, and discouraged preacher?" All of those inherent moods had caused my family to walk on eggshells at different times. Karen, of course, accepted my apology, and we cried out to God together.

I then called a very close friend named Jim Hennesy. I

asked him to pray with me to continue to walk in freedom. I felt this was critical to my personal freedom. Jim listened to me as I admitted my battle, and he told me of his own war and how he had decided to walk in freedom.

That day on the battlefield of Gettysburg, I had experienced a civil war. The battle was between two entities called flesh versus spirit. I confronted not only my past and present, but also my future. I decided that I would no longer be a victim of Belial. Worthlessness began to lose its foothold in my life.

I finally decided I would give God my pain. The enemy would absolutely love for each of us to live a life of secret pain, as he knows the most dangerous Christian is one that is whole. God is waiting on us to throw Him our pain! It is so easy to play the victim card and spend your life blaming everyone else. Sure, each of us has been wronged in one way or another, but we must confront the inner self. Victory in the Spirit comes most gracefully when we hide away and deal with what I call the enemy within.

> "I would rather be unqualified, because Jesus doesn't call the qualified; He qualifies the called. I want to be qualified by Jesus to do the work for His kingdom."
> —Elisabeth Saffell, 22, ministry student, Brooksville, FL

The Battle of Self

Anyone who has ever been used by God has had to fight the battle of self. The Book of James confronts this inner war head-on:

> Where do wars and fights among you come from? Do they not come from your lusts that war in your body? You lust and do not have, so you kill. You desire to have and cannot obtain. You fight and war. Yet you do

not have, because you do not ask. You ask, and do not receive, because you ask amiss, that you may spend it on your passions.

—James 4:1–3, mev

James doesn't hold back in this powerful proverb of the New Testament. He lets us know that we are our own biggest threat to freedom.

The apostle Paul agrees, telling us about his private battle with something he struggled to conquer:

> Because of the extravagance of those revelations, and so I wouldn't get a big head, I was given the gift of a handicap to keep me in constant touch with my limitations. Satan's angel did his best to get me down; what he in fact did was push me to my knees. No danger then of walking around high and mighty! At first I didn't think of it as a gift, and begged God to remove it. Three times I did that, and then he told me, My grace is enough; it's all you need. My strength comes into its own in your weakness. Once I heard that, I was glad to let it happen. I quit focusing on the handicap and began appreciating the gift. It was a case of Christ's strength moving in on my weakness. Now I take limitations in stride, and with good cheer, these limitations that cut me down to size—abuse, accidents, opposition, bad breaks. I just let Christ take over! And so the weaker I get, the stronger I become.
>
> —2 Corinthians 12:7–10, The Message

He was declaring that this handicap that was meant to hold him back actually made him more effective. So again, what should disqualify us actually qualifies us!

God has not called you to walk in defeat, failure, depression, fear, or insecurity. He has called you to rise up as a child of the King. He calls you valuable.

> What's the price of two or three pet canaries? Some loose change, right? But God never overlooks a single

one. And he pays even greater attention to you, down to the last detail—even numbering the hairs on your head! So don't be intimidated by all this bully talk. You're worth more than a million canaries.

—LUKE 12:6–7, THE MESSAGE

We must realize that when others determine our value, we will eventually be sold off as a cheap piece of compromise. When we feel worthless is when the enemy will sneak in and we begin to live a life of compromise.

> "The unqualified is content with weakness, insults, distress, persecutions, and difficulties for Christ's sake. For His power works best in weakness."
>
> —Rich Perry, 21, ministry student, Richmond, VA

The enemy will do everything he can to disqualify you. Romans 7:11 says, "For sin, seizing the opportunity afforded by the commandment, deceived me, and through the commandment put me to death." So you mess up, and suddenly you feel worthless. Yet God still screams, "You're valuable!" If you are worthless, then why did He die for you?

A Powerful Promise Awaits

Do you know what happens when you take a stand against Belial? Adoption!

In 2 Corinthians 6 Paul takes us one step further by instructing us to be separate from the world, and with that separation comes a powerful promise:

> Therefore, "Come out from among them and be separate, says the Lord. Do not touch what is unclean, and I will receive you. I will be a Father to you, and you shall be My sons and daughters, says the Lord Almighty."
>
> —2 CORINTHIANS 6:17–18, MEV

Not only should we guard against the wrong yokes and defeat Belial, but we also must be separated from the world and its influence. In doing so, God says we will be accepted as His children. That is why Jesus promised in John 14:18–20, "I will not leave you orphaned. I'm coming back. In just a little while the world will no longer see me, but you're going to see me because I am alive and you're about to come alive. At that moment you will know absolutely that I'm in my Father, and you're in me, and I'm in you" (THE MESSAGE).

God declares you are a part of Him. That means God birthed you! He has chosen you as His child. People, opinions, and platforms do not determine your value, but rather our God who calls you His does! Will you take the path of separation from the world, the enemy of your soul, and your own flesh to receive this incredible promise?

Chapter 7

REHIRING THE HOLY SPIRIT

> "The unqualified are those who may not meet the proper requirements or qualifications that please men. They, in turn, are often better suited to be God pleasers. What seems to be their weakness, in reality, becomes their strength. Their message will help put others' faith in the power of God and not in the wisdom of men."
>
> —Greg DeVries, author and pastor, The Well Family Worship Center, Scottsboro, AL

OR MUCH OF my life I have felt unqualified as a leader in the kingdom of God. Whether I was working as a youth pastor, an evangelist, a lead pastor, or an author, I have always known that without the help of my closest adviser and guide, I would not make it! This adviser has been with me my whole life. He was with me as a boy when I was lost in a ruthless world. He was with me when I heard the call of God at a children's camp during a puppet show where I was a sixteen-year-old camp worker. He was with me when I was running from God. In fact, He drove me crazy. It seemed in every direction I went, He was waiting for me. He was with me when I met my wife. He was with me when I held my son and my daughter for the first time. I have shared so many memories with this dear friend. He has guided me as a husband, father, son, pastor, and evangelist. Whether it was when I lost my sister or held my first book in my hands, He was there.

I, of course, speak of the Holy Spirit.

Recently while praying, I heard God say to me, "Son, why is the church ashamed of My Spirit? Why has My Spirit been fired from most churches? Do they not realize that they cannot do true ministry without Me?" As I prayed, I began to ponder what the Lord had asked. For years I have cried out for revival to hit America. I believe that revival happens when God gets so sick and tired of being misrepresented that He shows up. I believe it also happens when the church cries out for intervention from above because it doesn't want to continue through the doorway of mediocrity and often-plagiarized self-help sermonettes with no power.

> "Being aware that you are unqualified is the greatest revelation you can have about yourself. It's the place you realize that despite all your inadequacies, insecurities, fears, and failures, God still takes pleasure in using you to accomplish His plans. The focus then becomes less on self and more on Jesus, which is exactly where it should be."
>
> —Tim Cravens, associate pastor, Santa Cruz, CA

This generation wants to see the outpouring of the Holy Spirit. The spiritual leaders of today act as if they have out-grown the move of God. To decide that this generation is not worthy of the same supernatural encounter you once had as a youth means the death of tomorrow's church! To decide that we must keep the passionate in the back rooms and back rows of churches means a slow death. We must not relegate the moves of God to retreats, encounters, and youth services. It will be the undignified who awaken the unqualified.

We have gotten so good at watering down the blood of Jesus in our messages that it now represents a pink slip for the firing of the Holy Spirit. He has been fired from many churches and places of worship and ostracized as too intrusive and too disruptive. Maybe He is forced to fly under the radar, living in the gymnasiums of youth services, the Bible studies of homes, and encounter weekends twice a year, because He has caused more upheaval than any person in history.

Listen to me, unqualified! You will never accomplish anything without the power of the Holy Spirit. Go ahead and let the intellectual and spiritually dry theologians of the day lead with their man-driven knowledge, but you and I must be inhabited by the third Person of the Trinity. God is moving through those of us who still allow Him to be God! For those who do not believe in the anointing at work in our lives, I need only to point them to this verse:

> Little children, it is the last hour. As you have heard that the antichrist will come, even now there are many antichrists. By this we know that it is the last hour. They went out from us, but they were not of us, for if they had been of us, they would no doubt have remained with us. But they went out, revealing that none of them were of us. But you have an anointing from the Holy One, and you know all things.
> —1 John 2:18–20, mev

I believe there are many who are more impressed with the aesthetics of the church than the anointing in the church. We often put more importance on the lighting, stage set, and sound than we do on crying out for an encounter with God. But great programs, warm bodies, and full offering buckets have never transformed the hurting. It is the Holy Spirit who does the work.

I believe it's time to hire Him back.

The Three Categories of the Church

The American church, as I see it, is presently divided into three main categories.

1. The modern charismatic and Pentecostal churches

These churches are alive and still believe in the miraculous. God is not placed in a box, and lives are renewed often by powerful worship, messages of truth, and altar experiences. Many times these churches do a great job at launching multisites, apostolically, with sons and daughters from the house and vision. These churches invite the gifts of the Spirit to be in action. They are very good at promoting family values and reciting 1 Corinthians 12 and 14 concerning the gifts of the Spirit. These churches often focus on helping the financially strapped in their churches as well as other mission opportunities in their communities.

However, understanding and spiritual order are often lost in the noise of a Spirit-led church service. The leadership often removes accountability and oversight in the name of apostolic freedom. The leadership can be controlling in the name of being apostolic. If accountability is not put in place, these churches can become a breeding ground for self-seeking leaders who indulge in material wealth and the perversions of the flesh. These churches often do not have strong outreach programs.

2. The modern evangelical church

These churches are usually strong in the Word of God and are usually mission-minded and socially driven. They are very good at growing small churches into megachurches and manufacturing multisites, and they are more entrepreneurial than apostolic. These churches are very good at promoting the Romans 12 works of grace. They are usually great at supporting overseas missions.

However, these churches often preach a grace message that

brings with it very little repentance. Rarely do these churches experience a deep move of God. They are often better at reciting the past than where God is taking them in the future. Their church services usually do not allow opportunities for lives to encounter the Holy Spirit. Leadership can often be more personality-driven and organization-driven than driven by lives living under the anointing of the Holy Spirit.

3. The seeker-driven model

These churches are very good at bringing lost sheep home. They have an ability to remove religious mind-sets that have hindered people. These churches usually have a combination of both the charismatic and evangelical. Worship is usually very lively. These churches most often believe in a strong grace message combined with the Word of Faith message. They are very good at launching multisites. They are often very good at creating community via small groups. The outreaches organized by these churches often are better than the local community government can provide. Sometimes (though not always) these churches cherry-pick the 1 Corinthians 12 and 14 gifts of the Spirit as well as the Romans 12 works of grace.

However, spiritual depth in these congregations is not as important as community. Often the sermons contain very little Scripture because life stories and anecdotes dominate the messages. Encounters with God are frowned upon as too intrusive. Very little deliverance takes place in the lives of these churches, and when it does, it is usually in a twice-a-year retreat. Holiness is rarely preached from the pulpits because it is counterproductive to population growth.

Now I am very sure some of what I have written here can be debated. Remember, this is just my spectator's opinion, but I believe there's great merit to this opinion, and I've often wondered if it's possible to take all of the positives from the three church models and combine them. If so, I believe we could win the world. What if we allowed the

Holy Spirit to move, combined that with learning how to reach the lost with a message of hope, allowed the lost to get free, and then caught a vision for our cities? That definitely seems like a run-on sentence, but I'm willing to be grammatically incorrect to see the church rise up and represent heaven invading earth!

Do We Really Need the Holy Spirit?

Recently a well-known television evangelist made the statement, "The Holy Spirit does not convict the believer of sin but of his righteousness in Christ!" There is some truth in this statement, but it is also very misleading. Yes, the Holy Spirit brings us into righteousness with God, but none of us should ever get to a place where we no longer have conviction at work in our lives. It is the Holy Spirit that brings conviction! Jesus said, "When he comes, he will prove the world to be in the wrong about sin and righteousness and judgment" (John 16:8).

The same minister also made this statement: "The work of the Holy Spirit is no longer needed." This is an absolute farce. The work of the Holy Spirit will always be with us. It is the Holy Spirit that leads us to truth. In John 16:12–15 Jesus also said:

> I still have many things to tell you, but you can't handle them now. But when the Friend comes, the Spirit of the Truth, he will take you by the hand and guide you into all the truth there is. He won't draw attention to himself, but will make sense out of what is about to happen and, indeed, out of all that I have done and said. He will honor me; he will take from me and deliver it to you. Everything the Father has is also mine. That is why I've said, "He takes from me and delivers to you."
>
> —THE MESSAGE

The moment the church decides to be quiet and stop declaring the truth is the same moment we become irrelevant. It is also the Holy Spirit who gives us the power to declare the truth in the first place, as Jesus instructed His disciples in Acts 1:8: "But you will receive power when the Holy Spirit comes on you; and you will be my witnesses."

The Holy Spirit convicts us of sin. The work of the Holy Spirit advocates on our behalf. The Holy Spirit gives us power. The Holy Spirit also comforts us when we are in need. Do we need the Holy Spirit? Without a doubt.

In fact, we *must* have the work of the Holy Spirit! We are now witnessing the invasion of humanism at every level. Many sermons represent a do-it-yourself, pump-you-up, you-can-do-it message of recycled humanism. I'm convinced that if the Holy Spirit is forced out of the church, the church will be nothing more than a social club that brings very little change. For too long many have listened to the opinion of the crowds, the committees, and the comfortable when it comes to allowing the movement of the Spirit in our churches. But again, God never called us to fit in!

> The world is unprincipled. It's dog-eat-dog out there! The world doesn't fight fair. But we don't live or fight our battles that way—never have and never will. The tools of our trade aren't for marketing or manipulation, but they are for demolishing that entire massively corrupt culture. We use our powerful God-tools for smashing warped philosophies, tearing down barriers erected against the truth of God, fitting every loose thought and emotion and impulse into the structure of life shaped by Christ. Our tools are ready at hand for clearing the ground of every obstruction and building lives of obedience into maturity.
> —2 CORINTHIANS 10:3–6, THE MESSAGE

When we said, "I have decided to follow Jesus," it wasn't by the leading of a mob but by the love of a King. Remember, the mob crucified Jesus! If we continue to create a benign label that determines what flavor we enjoy when we eat at the table of the Lord, we will turn God into nothing more than an idol on our shelves whose belly we rub when we have a need. We must get back to our first love.

For decades we have tried preaching compassion without truth in order to fill pews. This will only gather the goats while the sheep continue to stray! People are hurting. They are looking for real answers and real encounters. This will never happen if we do not allow the Spirit of God to move. We are living in a day where nice messages and sweet services allow the demons to relax and make fodder of God's people. It is time for the sons of God to rise up.

> "The unqualified are being forged in winepresses like Gideon, are being trained for the Goliath of their generation while tending sheep, are overcoming being overlooked during the day so they can answer the call for the last harvest that brings in the night."
>
> —Juan Rivera, pastor, Youngstown, OH

I believe our nation is in travail for the sons of God to be revealed. As Paul wrote, "We know that the whole creation has been groaning as in the pains of childbirth right up to the present time. Not only so, but we ourselves, who have the firstfruits of the Spirit, groan inwardly as we wait eagerly for our adoption to sonship, the redemption of our bodies" (Rom. 8:22–23). Those who will spiritually change our nation will be those who are empowered to do the mighty deeds of the Lord.

I believe this is the unqualified! They will deal with spiritual wickedness of the day and those who commit treason against the kingdom. Sin is running rampant not only in our communities and schools, but also in our powerless churches. Could it be that the One we have so desperately tried to quiet in our massive churches and Christian gatherings is the One who could transform our cities? I love what evangelist Reinhard Bonnke once said: "The power of God is not an accessory to the gospel. It is all power!"

The Light of Truth

We are called to be the messengers of light, and our churches should be the lighthouses in the storms. The lights of many churches have grown very dim. Jesus said, "Neither do people light a lamp and put it under a bowl. Instead they put it on its stand, and it gives light to everyone in the house" (Matt. 5:15). We are the light in the darkness that leads others to safety.

I believe we are living in very dark times. Not just because the very concept of marriage is under attack. Not just because the culture is rewriting God's Word for pleasure of self. Not just because the culture is a lot louder than the church. Rather, because culture is now deciding what the church can say and do.

Depravity is now leading the conversations concerning what we can call sin. For example, the most hated chapter in many social circles today is Romans 1. This is the chapter the apostle Paul wrote that condemns homosexuality. Look what Paul wrote concerning the mind-set of the day. I believe this applies right now:

> Furthermore, just as they did not think it worthwhile to retain the knowledge of God, so God gave them over to a depraved mind, so that they do what ought not to be done.
> —ROMANS 1:28

The term *depraved* means "reprobate mind." This means a mind that is now "devoid of all true knowledge and judgment."[1] I never believed this verse could apply to the church until I realized some churches now teach sexual perversion is fine as long as two people believe they love each other.

This is an example of what I call our compassion crisis. Churches have come to so deeply love people's flesh that they are afraid to talk with them concerning their souls. To say we love people so much that we don't want to offend them is actually not showing them love at all. A person's eternal soul will long outlast their habitation in your church. If you fall into the trap of not declaring the truth, you will disqualify your voice. God has not called you to join the choir of "sin with no consequence" but rather to declare truth with God's love and freedom.

You must stand firm when the voices of fear overwhelm you. Ignore the lies of this world and be a truth teller! John 8:32 declares, "Then you will know the truth, and the truth will set you free." The soul needs to be told the truth. That is why we must allow the Holy Spirit to transform lives. We must love people enough to tell them truth and then value them enough to lead them to the cross of redemption.

> Souls are saved by truthful witness and betrayed by the spread of lies.
> —PROVERBS 14:25, THE MESSAGE

You must allow the Holy Spirit to personally lead you to the truth in order to lead others to the truth. God will restore their souls. You cannot simply love someone into heaven; you must lead them to the cross of freedom and let the Holy Spirit do the work.

To say that certain biblical subjects are taboo in the church because we might offend someone makes our message impotent. If telling the truth of God's Word will lead to persecution, then this means God's Word was correct! Prophecy was fulfilled, according to Matthew 24:9: "Then you will be handed over to be persecuted and put to death, and you will be hated by all nations because of me."

We must never forget that Jesus died to redeem us from the tyranny of culture, so we must now carry our cross publicly. Every Christian must ask himself, "Am I willing to be shamed for the truth, or will I be cheered for the cultural lie?" Truth doesn't bow! We must guard our lives or the sin we condone will overtake us. Soon we will hear from pulpits that it is all right to live like the world. To believe you can partake in the lifestyle of those you're called to win means you're being seduced by that from which Jesus set you free!

> "The unqualified are the sons and daughters the world has discarded but that God often uses. They rise from the ashes of pain and rejection, often shaping history."
> —Romeo Billups, youth pastor, Lagrange, GA

You might say, "But it's not popular to be so honest!" When we stand before Jesus, He will not ask who we knew or who we hung out with, but rather if we took up our cross. When we decide to make Christ famous, it doesn't come with a promise of personal popularity. Actually, we decrease that He might increase! We must stand for truth.

> So here's what I want you to do, God helping you: Take your everyday, ordinary life—your sleeping, eating, going-to-work, and walking-around life—and place it before God as an offering. Embracing what God does for you is the best thing you can do for him. Don't become so well-adjusted to your culture that you fit into it without even thinking. Instead, fix your attention on God. You'll be changed from the inside out. Readily recognize what he wants from you, and quickly respond to it. Unlike the culture around you, always dragging you down to its level of immaturity,

God brings the best out of you, develops well-formed maturity in you.

—ROMANS 12:1–2, THE MESSAGE

An Interview With the Holy Spirit

As I mentioned in chapter 1, I believe that unless the Holy Spirit moves once again across our nation, we are doomed to destruction. As I write this chapter, I hear in my spirit the cry of 2 Chronicles 7:14: "If my people, who are called by my name, will humble themselves and pray and seek my face and turn from their wicked ways, then I will hear from heaven, and I will forgive their sin and will heal their land."

We need to rehire the Holy Spirit in our churches.

However, if we are going to do this effectively, we're going to need to ask Him some pretty direct questions. I believe that if we were to sit down with the Holy Spirit to ask Him those questions, He would answer them directly from the Bible.

Here's an example of how that interview might go:

When people say the Holy Spirit brings too much conviction to the church, how would You reply?

Galatians 5:16 says that if we walk in the Spirit, we will not fulfill our own lust.

Hebrews 10:15 tells us that the Holy Spirit is a witness of our lives.

What about those who do not want the work of the Holy Spirit?

Ephesians 4:30 warns us not to grieve the Holy Spirit.

First Thessalonians 5:19 again warns us not to quench the Holy Spirit.

Do You, the Holy Spirit, make Your home in us?

First Corinthians 3:16 tells us we are the temple of God and He dwells in us.

First Corinthians 6:19 says our body is the temple of the Holy Spirit.

What should we do with You, the Holy Spirit, in our lives?

Second Timothy 1:14 instructs us to guard, through the Holy Spirit, the treasure inside of us.

Are the gifts of the Holy Spirit real?

First Corinthians 12:13 says that by one Spirit we are all baptized into one body.

First Corinthians 12:7–11 describes, in detail, the gifts:

> Now to each one the manifestation of the Spirit is given for the common good. To one there is given through the Spirit a message of wisdom, to another a message of knowledge by means of the same Spirit, to another faith by the same Spirit, to another gifts of healing by that one Spirit, to another miraculous powers, to another prophecy, to another distinguishing between spirits, to another speaking in different kinds of tongues, and to still another the interpretation of tongues. All these are the work of one and the same Spirit, and he distributes them to each one, just as he determines.

First Corinthians 14:1 says to eagerly desire the gifts of the Spirit.

First Corinthians 14:3 says the one who prophesies speaks to people for their strengthening, encouraging, and comforting.

First Corinthians 14:22 says tongues are a sign to the unbeliever.

First Corinthians 14:40 tells us all of the gifts are done in order.

Should we desire more of the Holy Spirit?

Ephesians 5:18 emphatically says to be filled with the Holy Spirit.

Galatians 5:22–23 describes the fruit grown by the Spirit: "But the fruit of the Spirit is love, joy, peace, forbearance, kindness, goodness, faithfulness, gentleness and self-control. Against such things there is no law."

Romans 8:14 says if we are led by the Spirit, we are sons of God.

What is the Holy Spirit saying to the church today?

Revelation 22:17 says, "The Spirit and the bride say, 'Come.' Let him who hears say, 'Come.' Let him who is thirsty come. Let him who desires take the water of life freely" (MEV).

What is the Holy Spirit's future plan for the last days?

Joel 2:28 and Acts 2:17 both say the following: "And afterward, I will pour out my Spirit on all people. Your sons and daughters will prophesy, your old men will dream dreams, your young men will see visions."

How can the Holy Spirit help those who are searching and in pain?

By reminding them things aren't over yet, as Romans 5:3–5 (THE MESSAGE) promises:

> There's more to come: We continue to shout our praise even when we're hemmed in with troubles, because we know how troubles can develop passionate patience in us, and how that patience in turn forges the tempered steel of virtue, keeping us alert for whatever God will do next. In alert expectancy such as this, we're never left feeling shortchanged. Quite the contrary—we can't round up enough containers to hold everything God generously pours into our lives through the Holy Spirit!

Can the Holy Spirit use those of us who have failed so many times?

Yes. First Timothy 1:12–16 gives the example of Paul, who says of himself:

I thank Christ Jesus our Lord, who has enabled me, because He counted me faithful and appointed me to the ministry. I was previously a blasphemer, and a persecutor, and an insolent man. But I was shown mercy, because I did it ignorantly in unbelief. The grace of our Lord overflowed with the faith and love which is in Christ Jesus. This is a faithful saying and worthy of all acceptance, that Christ Jesus came into the world to save sinners, of whom I am the worst. But I received mercy for this reason, that in me, first, Jesus Christ might show all patience, as an example to those who were to believe in Him for eternal life.

—MEV

What would the Holy Spirit say to the church today?

It can best be summed up by 2 Corinthians 6:14–18 (The Message), which gives this advice:

Don't become partners with those who reject God. How can you make a partnership out of right and wrong? That's not partnership; that's war. Is light best friends with dark? Does Christ go strolling with the Devil? Do trust and mistrust hold hands? Who would think of setting up pagan idols in God's holy Temple? But that is exactly what we are, each of us a temple in whom God lives. God himself put it this way: "I'll live in them, move into them; I'll be their God and they'll be my people. So leave the corruption and compromise; leave it for good," says God. "Don't link up with those who will pollute you. I want you all for myself. I'll be a Father to you; you'll be sons and daughters to me." The Word of the Master, God.

There's Only One Way Forward

I will close this chapter with a final question for the unqualified. Is it possible to do what you are called to do without the habitation and partnership of the Holy Spirit in your life? I think the answer is a resounding no.

I challenge the church to hire the Holy Spirit back. What do we have to lose? Everything!

"The unqualified are those who have been disqualified not just by people but sometimes life itself. How do unlearned fishermen and an unforgiving tax collector turn the world upside down with revelation and unconditional love? Jesus took the unqualified and actually told them, 'You will do greater things than these.' What? The man whose writings are quoted and taught in churches maybe more than any other, the apostle Paul, would not even be qualified to be a door greeter in those same churches. Imprisoned, beaten, thrown out of towns, shipwrecked, stricken with disease, and formerly known to order the killing of some Christians! How? His own words give us the call of the unqualified: 'I did not come to you with persuasive words of man's wisdom but in power and demonstration of the Holy Ghost!' Even though his education could have qualified him to speak, he chose to follow Christ as the unqualified. This decision to be marked, not for his glory but the glory of God, made him unoffendable and impossible for the enemy to destroy. 'Paul, we will kill you'—to die is gain! 'We will release you'—to live is Christ! 'We will beat you'—I do not compare these present sufferings with the future glory! 'We will put you in jail'—OK, we will worship the Lord, the prisoners will be set free, the guards will be saved, and we will have a baptismal service! The unqualified become the untouchable remnant to establish and demonstrate the kingdom of God on the earth to usher in His rule and reign!"

—Scott Ethridge, pastor, Healing Place Church, Shreveport, LA

Chapter 8

WILDERNESS WANDERERS

"The unqualified are the hidden trophies of heaven. They are hope dealers and risk takers with unwavering obedience to the Word of God and reckless abandonment to the cause of Christ. Their battle cry is 'Courage!'—and courage often disguises itself as crazy!"

—Chilly Chilton, pastor, Detroit, MI

ONE MORNING YEARS ago while praying, I said, "Lord, why do I feel as though I am alone during this season? Have You left me?" Then I heard the Lord say, "Pat, I have gone to another level, and I am waiting on you to get here!" As I look back, I realize I was in a season of preparation for a new level of walking in the Spirit.

The lesson of this chapter is: don't ask God to anoint you for a new season if you aren't willing to walk a path less traveled by others. We'll speak in this chapter of the hidden times and the dark times we often walk as Christians.

> Who among you fears the LORD, who obeys the voice of His servant, who walks in darkness and has no light? Let him trust in the name of the LORD, and rely upon his God.
> —ISAIAH 50:10, MEV

We must realize, first of all, that God is nocturnal. He can see you in the dark. The unqualified are the ones most in need of qualification from God and desertion from man. Why is that? It's simple. When man ignores or leaves you, you have no choice but to seek out God for the answers.

Also, I want to remove the myth that people arrive on the scene ready to change the world. If that were the case, then the unqualified may as well quit before the journey begins. Those of us who are unqualified know we will never experience instantaneous notoriety or fame. That is the way man often does it, but not God. Man always props people up, but God raises people up who are humbled by His love, joy, and freedom.

As the voice of God to this world, it is vitally important that the unqualified understand their journey is much more important than their arrival. What do I mean? It is in the journey of preparation that the foundation for greatness is laid. We do not very often hear of the journey because we are so enamored with the finished product that glimmers on the stage. But without walking through the God-ordained process of development He has for each of us, we will never become the vessel God can use.

You cannot skip any of the steps. There is always a process!

Jesus understood this need for process. He could have shown up on the earth as the mighty Lord who commanded the world to bow and obey, but He himself went through the process. He came in the form of a baby, wrapped in flesh and exposed to the elements of a dangerous world.

> Think of yourselves the way Christ Jesus thought of himself. He had equal status with God but didn't think so much of himself that he had to cling to the advantages of that status no matter what. Not at all. When the time came, he set aside the privileges of deity and took on the status of a slave, became human! Having become human, he stayed human. It was an incredibly

humbling process. He didn't claim special privileges. Instead, he lived a selfless, obedient life and then died a selfless, obedient death—and the worst kind of death at that—a crucifixion.
—PHILIPPIANS 2:5–8, THE MESSAGE

As you can see, it was the process that made Jesus all the more ready to be our righteous and holy Lamb.

The Two Necessary Places

What many fail to realize is that the stage of undeveloped ministry is where the scars of past failures can shine the brightest. If you have not walked the wilderness journey, then you will never really be a voice but rather an echo of what you could and should have been. Your greatest moments of spiritual training will not come while standing on the platform of ministry or in the office of the elite but in the cave and in the wilderness. I have never met anyone who has been greatly used of God who did not first have to visit these two places.

These two places are not usually envisioned when we accept the call to be used of God. Nevertheless, without these places you may never arrive. Until you become a cave dweller and wilderness walker, you will never understand the depths of God's love and His infinite wisdom for your life.

The cave

The cave is the place of encounter, and the wilderness is the place of desperation. The psalmist spoke of the cave experience in Psalm 31:3–5, "You're my cave to hide in, my cliff to climb. Be my safe leader, be my true mountain guide. Free me from hidden traps; I want to hide in you. I've put my life in your hands. You won't drop me, you'll never let me down" (THE MESSAGE).

In my last book, *I Am Remnant*, I wrote briefly about the

cave in a chapter called "The Oscar Goes to…," where I shared the following:

> It is in the cave that God can reshape our thinking and remold our hearts. There have been times where I have prayed that God would put me in His cave because these are the times that He speaks the loudest and draws me back to my priorities.
>
> I call it a cave because God used the cave many times to rescue and restore His leaders. He protected His people in caves in 1 Samuel 13:6: "When the men of Israel saw that their situation was critical and that their army was hard pressed, they hid in caves and thickets, among the rocks, and in pits and cisterns" (NIV). It was in the cave experience that David began the process of building his army (1 Sam. 22:1). This is where Moses was hidden when God's glory passed by and gave him the revelation to write the first five books of the Bible (Exod. 33:22). It is in the cave that Elijah had God's glory pass by in 1 Kings 19:11. This is where Elijah discerned that God was not in the wind, the earthquake, or the fire, but in the whisper.
>
> We too must get back to the cave. It is in the cave God speaks to his warrior.[1]

The wilderness

God uses the cave to secure you in Him, but the wilderness is the place God separates you from the world. The cave is where you hide, but the wilderness is where you defeat the enemies that lie in wait for you. I have learned that without the cave, you may never learn to listen for the voice of God, but without the wilderness, you may never learn to desire the depths of God. The cave is a wonderful place of encounter, but it is in the wilderness that God develops your identity, calling, and, most of all, your character. In the wilderness you will find that your greatest enemy is the vision that burns within you, and your best friend becomes the altar of hope. The wilderness can also be described as a desert experience.

I must tell you that the times I have walked through the wilderness season will never supersede my cave experiences and vice versa, because each place is designed to mold you in a different way. The wilderness, though, is the place where I decided I can't quit. I knew God would lead me out if I would hold on to Him.

There are eight reasons for the wilderness:

1. To destroy bondage
2. To remove that which you have depended on for so long
3. To restart a fire
4. To restore a burden
5. To develop your calling
6. To restore the joy of your salvation
7. To receive the joy of the mantle God has for you
8. To restore your intimacy with the Father

In 1993 I read a powerful book by John Bevere called *Victory in the Wilderness*. I had only been in the ministry for about two years, but this book touched me deeply! Here is just a small portion that helps explain the wilderness:

> Such maturity of character is developed in us by God when we are in the wilderness. The wilderness is where the fruit of the Spirit is cultivated. Watered by the intense desire to know Him, we seek to walk as He walks. Paul's goal was not to build a huge ministry, but to know the Lord Jesus intimately and, above all else, to please Him!
>
> The wilderness is a dry place. It may be dry spiritually, financially, socially, or physically. It is here

that God gives "daily bread," not "abundance of things." He meets our needs in this time—not necessarily our wants. The purpose of the wilderness—to purify us. Our pursuit is to be His *heart,* not His *provision.* Then when we come into abundant times, we won't forget that it was the Lord, our God, Who gave us abundance in order to establish His covenant (Deuteronomy 8:2–18).[2]

> "Men love their résumés full of their qualifications. The unqualified simply need to hear God's voice."
>
> —Landon Schott, president, REVtv.com

Three Types of Wilderness

There are three kinds of wilderness journeys we can encounter along the way. Let's review them now.

1. The Wilderness of Isolation

The wilderness has the ability to make you feel invisible and all alone. It's the place you scream and cry out but no one hears your cries. No one, that is, except God. This is God's way of making sure that He has all of your attention. God will allow you to wander until you cry out for Him. Whether you are living in a life of sin or God is breaking things off of you that will hold you back in the future, He waits for you to cry out. It is in the alone place that you cry out for God's help. Psalm 25:16 says, "Look at me and help me! I'm all alone and in big trouble" (THE MESSAGE).

In this season of obscurity we realize God is our source and strength. Have you ever been in a massive crowd and yet felt all alone? I believe we've all felt that way on one occasion or another. The greatest revelations of the love of God do not come when everyone is cheering you on, knows your name, or acclaims your works before others. No, it is when you turn to your right and left and those spaces are empty of human presence that God shows up.

> As I sink in despair, my spirit ebbing away, you know how I'm feeling, know the danger I'm in, the traps hidden in my path. Look right, look left—there's not a soul who cares what happens! I'm up against it, with no exit—bereft, left alone. I cry out, GOD, call out: "You're my last chance, my only hope for life!" Oh listen, please listen; I've never been this low. Rescue me from those who are hunting me down; I'm no match for them. Get me out of this dungeon so I can thank you in public. Your people will form a circle around me and you'll bring me showers of blessing!
> —PSALM 142:3–7, THE MESSAGE

The wilderness of isolation is the place where God restores your testimony of His awesome deliverance. Without the wilderness, you will never understand the power of deliverance.

God wants you to know He hasn't left! He is using this season to call you back to Him. He is a selfish God that wants all of your attention. He will show you the way out. He doesn't need your permission to be faithful, but what He does need is your obedience to bring the end result. It is in the wilderness that your perception changes and your desire for God increases. God will isolate you to help you break free of the old and experience Him anew!

> Forget about what's happened; don't keep going over old history. Be alert, be present. I'm about to do something brand-new. It's bursting out! Don't you see it? There it is! I'm making a road through the desert, rivers in the badlands.
> —ISAIAH 43:18–19, THE MESSAGE

To give you an idea of the isolating nature of the wilderness, I'll share a story with you from several years ago, when I went to North Dakota to minister. After a few days of ministry the pastor of the church where I was ministering went with me on a four-hour journey to South Dakota for a church service. The ride was pretty uneventful until, suddenly, in the middle of the dry plains we came upon the Badlands. It was full of majestic mountains that were painted in pastel colors, so picturesque and beautiful.

The pastor said to me, "This place is beautiful, but this is the last place we want to break down." It was obvious why he said that; there was not another person or car in sight. If we were to break down, it would be a long, cold night. I thought to myself, "Why on earth would we come this direction?" but I realized we had to go through the Badlands to get to the place we were ministering that night in South Dakota.

In other words, many times you cannot escape where you must walk in order to stand on the platform that awaits you on the other side. We do not get to pick our wilderness as if we are sitting with a travel agent planning our next vacation. The wilderness has a way of suddenly appearing on our map.

But the great thing about a God wilderness is that He never makes us walk it alone. The psalmist declared, "Even when the way goes through Death Valley, I'm not afraid when you walk at my side. Your trusty shepherd's crook makes me feel secure" (Ps. 23:4, THE MESSAGE).

2. The Wilderness of Confrontation

Moses lived in the wilderness for forty years, and this prepared him to lead the people out of Egypt. He understood that it was while he was invisible to the world that he met a visible God in a burning bush. This gave him strength to stand against Pharaoh. Hebrews 11:27 says, "By faith he left Egypt, not fearing the king's anger; he persevered because he saw him who is invisible."

In the wilderness you find out what you're made of. The Bible says that soon after winning their freedom from Pharaoh, the Israelites began to complain and whine—and what should have been a short journey to the Promised Land ended up being a forty-year wandering journey through wilderness. The children of Israel wandered because they were a rebellious people. They often forgot what God had done on their behalf. Psalm 106:13–14 speaks of this: "But they soon forgot what he had done and did not wait for his plan to unfold. In the desert they gave in to their craving; in the wilderness they put God to the test."

Over and over God would confront the children of Israel. It wasn't until a new generation arose that God brought them into the Promised Land. In fact, the only ones left of that generation were Joshua and Caleb!

How you handle your wilderness will determine if God has to bring forth a new generation of leaders. It is also in the wilderness that God often brings forth new leadership in our lives.

3. The Wilderness of Consecration

God has called us to be consecrated. The word *consecrated* means "to be separate or set apart." I have always said that the greater the anointing, the greater the isolation—and you will never get anointed until you are forgotten. Just ask Moses, David, or, most of all, Jesus. Jesus disappeared from the age of twelve to thirty. Where did He go during that time? We know that Luke 2:52 says, "And Jesus grew in wisdom and stature, and in favor with God and man." Then—poof!—He was gone from the radar. For the next eighteen years He would serve His family, maybe do construction, and seek the heart of His Father.

There is no biblical account of Jesus again until the age of thirty, when He showed up to be baptized by John the Baptist in the Jordan River. This was His public consecration for becoming a priest, as public baptism had to take place for Jesus to serve as a priest. This was His moment. John 1:29 declares, "The next day John saw Jesus coming toward him and said, "Look, the Lamb of God, who takes away the sin of the world!" We know that when He was baptized in the water, the heavens opened and God said, "You are my Son, whom I love; with you I am well pleased" (Luke 3:22).

Now it was time for Jesus to start His ministry. After that type of introduction, He should hold a massive crusade, right? But what did Jesus do? He disappeared again! The Holy Spirit led Him into an epic battle with His oldest foe, Satan.

> Jesus, being filled with the Holy Spirit, returned from the Jordan and was led by the Spirit into the wilderness, being tempted by the devil for forty days. During those days He ate nothing. And when they were ended, He was hungry.
> —LUKE 4:1–2, MEV

This is powerful. Jesus understood that although you may be ready to free the world, you must first do battle with what you're freeing the world from. He would wander alone in obscurity for the next forty days. He would be thirsty and hungry to the point that His flesh was screaming for sustenance. Then, just as He felt as if He would die, He faced the three temptations.

Have you ever wondered why the temptations didn't come until the end of the forty days? I know I did until I realized it is easy to do battle when your physical needs are met. The real struggle takes place when you're famished and ready to sell your birthright, as Esau did for a pot of soup in Genesis 25.

Amazingly all three temptations brought against Jesus in the wilderness represent the three categories of sin we will battle in this world. First John 2:16 says, "For everything in the world—the lust of the flesh, the lust of the eyes, and the pride of life—comes not from the Father but from the world." When you enter your wilderness season—and you will—you must make up your mind to confront what will be waiting on you when you arrive on the stage.

The three temptations were:

1. Turn stones to bread. This temptation represents the lust of the flesh. The devil knew Jesus was starving in His flesh and said to Him, "If you are the Son of God, tell this stone to become bread." Jesus answered, "It is written: 'Man shall not live on bread alone'" (Luke 4:3–4). In modern terms, Jesus answered with, "You haven't got anything to offer me. God is my source, not you, Devil!"

2. Jump from the pinnacle of the Temple. This represents the pride of life. The devil challenged Jesus to prove His power and authority, leading Him to the highest point of the temple and saying, "'If you are the Son of God,' he said, 'throw yourself down from here. For it is written: "He will command his angels concerning you to guard you carefully; they will lift you up in their hands, so that you will not strike your foot against a stone."' Jesus answered, 'It is said: "Do not put the Lord your God to the test"'" (Luke 4:9–12). In modern terms, Jesus answered with, "Satan, you can't make me do a thing. I'm in charge. Back up, pal!"

3. Bow to receive the world. This temptation represents the lust of the eyes. This is where the devil tried to challenge Jesus's loyalty to God: "The devil led him up to a high place and showed him in an instant all the kingdoms of the world. And he said to him, 'I will give you all their authority and splendor; it has been given to me, and I can give it to anyone I want to. If you worship me, it will all be yours.' Jesus answered, 'It is written: "Worship the Lord your God and serve him only"'" (Luke 4:5–8). In modern terms, Jesus answered with, "You

will worship me, Satan! You can't give me what
I already have dominion over."

The enemy's goal is to always get you to choose flesh over
Spirit. But God has always got your back.

No temptation has taken you except what is common
to man. God is faithful, and He will not permit you to
be tempted above what you can endure, but will with
the temptation also make a way to escape, that you
may be able to bear it.
—1 Corinthians 10:13, mev

When the devil realized he had met his match, he left
Jesus alone in the wilderness—at least until he could find
a more "opportune time" (Luke 4:13). (He would wait to
bother Jesus until He was in a garden holding the weight of
our sin on His shoulders.)

But then the most amazing thing takes place. The angels
came and tended to the Savior of the world (Matt. 4:11)!
Even Jesus needed to be tended to after the wilderness.

Did you know that angels also minister to us? Early on
the morning of July 31, 2006, I experienced my first earthquake in Santa Cruz, California, where I had been ministering at a youth camp. It was just a small tremor, but it
awoke me from my sleep. I felt that the earthquake symbolized our ministry life during that season. We had just
decided to plant a church in Birmingham, Alabama, because
Karen and I felt we needed to pastor for a season. My son
was headed into the ninth grade, and it was time for Dad to
be home for a season. This would mean canceling our evan-
gelistic schedule and taking a major step of faith.

The excitement of planting a new work had passed, and
now the anxiety was beginning to settle in. We were only
three months from the launch, and the voice of the enemy
was growing louder by the day. I decided to get up and
spend some time in prayer after being awakened by the

earthquake. It was still very early in the morning, but the earthquake had rattled my nerves. During prayer I said, "God, I just need to know You're with me during this season. Please give me a sign." I know it is not wise to ask for signs, but I was desperate.

After prayer I began to get ready for the youth camp's morning service, where I would be speaking. As I stood in front of the mirror brushing my teeth, I saw something out of the corner of my eye. I turned to look, and suddenly I saw an angel standing in the corner of the room. The angel was probably nine feet tall, and he was dressed in armor. His wings were so high that they were bent downward at the tips because there wasn't enough room for them to fit. The angel was looking down toward me. Then he was gone. It was as quick as that.

The angel didn't say anything or make any motion. Then suddenly I heard God say to me, "I just wanted you to know We were here!" I stood frozen for what seemed like minutes, and I began to worship the Lord. The Bible tells me, "Are not all angels ministering spirits sent to serve those who will inherit salvation?" (Heb. 1:14). This should absolutely excite you and me. We're not alone. Psalm 34:6–7 says, "When I was desperate, I called out, and GOD got me out of a tight spot. GOD's angel sets up a circle of protection around us while we pray" (THE MESSAGE).

> "The unqualified is the secret one. The one whose voice is only loud in the prayer closet. The one with the well-worn keys to the secret place."
>
> —Josh Hawkins, youth pastor, Fort Wayne, IN

Now back to our story. You would think Jesus would take a sabbatical after those forty long days in the wilderness and the scene of temptation with His enemy. I mean, He had just done battle with every possible sin! That is why it says in Hebrews 4:15, "For we do not have a high priest who is unable to empathize with our weaknesses, but we have one who has been tempted in every way, just as we are—yet he did not sin." He was due for a vacation, right? Nope. Look what Jesus does next:

> Jesus returned in the power of the Spirit to Galilee. And His fame went throughout the surrounding region. He taught in their synagogues, being glorified by everyone.
> —LUKE 4:14–15, MEV

So often we want the reputation when we're not ready. We haven't conquered the flesh yet and so, eventually, the flesh will conquer us. But you will never lead when you're still battling with what is behind you. Selfish ambition will destroy the leader. But Jesus made Himself of no reputation. He didn't come and build His ministry. God gave Him everything He needed to touch the world. It was when He was powerful in the Spirit that His reputation began to spread.

Jesus taught us that we have the power to once and for all conquer the very things that sought to destroy us. It is in the wilderness of consecration that your hunger, vision, and flesh change to desire God more than what the devil has to offer.

Ten Guidelines for Surviving the Wilderness

If you are walking through a wilderness or desert, then I want to challenge you to hold on. Allow this season to make you so hungry and desperate for God that you become alive for Him.

Here are ten guidelines to help you survive this season:

1. Don't look back! There is a greater anointing ahead.

2. Don't regret, but instead dream for your next level.

3. Take the time to create a new vision for the next ten years and begin to pursue it.

4. Realize this is the place where the "should've beens" stop.

5. Remember that the attack that comes in the wilderness is a planned assault by the devil to make you think you're irrelevant—because, in fact, you're so very relevant.

6. Use this time to pursue sons and daughters God has called you to raise up.

7. Use this time to draw close to your spouse and family.

8. Grab your joy back by the horns and say, "I am not letting go."

9. Guard who you talk to! Only spiritual fathers and mothers understand.

10. Remember that in your wilderness, you will find a new wineskin.

And remember this psalm on your toughest day:

Don't raise your fist against High God. Don't raise your voice against Rock of Ages. He's the One from east to west; from desert to mountains, he's the One.

—PSALM 75:5–6, THE MESSAGE

SECTION III

DON'T GET DISQUALIFIED!

Chapter 9

THE EIGHT INSATIABLE
ABSOLUTES OF THE UNQUALIFIED

> "One encounter with God can change the direction and course of any individual. It's not affluence, it's not ability, and it's not about ambition. It's about being available for an encounter! I am that kid with no Pentecostal heritage, no affluence, and not much ability. But I was available for the encounter."
>
> —Al Force, district youth director, Assemblies of God, Peninsular Florida District

P
AT, YOU HAVE an honesty problem!"

Those were the words I heard from a dear friend many years ago when I first started ministry. They absolutely crushed me! Here was a guy I had invited to be a guest speaker at the church where I was a youth pastor in Indianapolis, Indiana. The church was a very large denominational church. Its very size and reputation were enough to make a résumé look good. The service had gone wonderfully. Surely I had impressed him with the size of the crowd. I thought that was a true sign of solid ministry.

Now this well-known youth communicator was sitting across from me at a Chili's restaurant getting in my stuff. Who did he think he was? I will tell you who he was. He was a true friend who loved me enough to be honest. For years dating back to my childhood I would embellish stories or stretch the truth. In the early years it was to get out of trouble or pass the buck. Sure, many times I would often get caught by my parents or teachers, but this didn't break the pattern of deception. Lying has the ability to even convince the liar this is what is best for the moment.

I had such deep insecurity that I felt I needed to add to things to get man's approval. This issue in my life had followed me into ministry. I often told people we drew larger crowds to our services than we actually did and would even embellish personal illustrations as I spoke. This pattern was so deeply rooted in my life that I didn't even realize I was doing it. This conversation with my friend would change me forever.

I went home that night to my church parsonage and wept through the night. And sometime between 2:00 and 4:00 a.m., I began the journey to freedom.

I couldn't help wondering how many times I had told lies to impress others. I remember calling my dad in the middle of the night and saying, "Dad, do you think I have an honesty problem?" He said, "Yes, but we all do until you decide the truth is better than a lie. Now get free and move forward!" I also woke my wife up and repented for this fatal flaw in my armor.

To say that I was free of that issue right then would be a lie. I have and will always have to check my facts when I say things. Over time it has become easier to be honest, though, because I find it easier to say the truth than be embarrassed by chasing down a lie.

I have learned that you can always tell if someone has an honesty problem by the fact that they continually sensationalize the most simplistic moments. The Bible speaks strongly about walking in honesty. Proverbs 12:22 says, "The LORD detests lying lips, but he delights in people who are trustworthy."

You must despise the day when there is no one around to speak truth into your life. We must have those who love us enough to not only confront us, but also to help guide us into freedom. I honor that friend who decided to love me enough to be honest. Most of all, I praise God that He loved me enough to send that friend to me. I often say, "I think God puts up with us because He knows our end result!"

Winston Churchill once said, "When the eagles are silent, the parrots begin to jabber."[1] My prayer for you is that eagles will rise up and speak truth into your life. Until we realize choices have consequences, we will continually push the boundaries of reality. Jesus warned us about our words in Matthew 12:36–37: "But I say to you that for every idle word men may speak, they will give account of it in the day of judgment. For by your words you will be justified, and by your words you will be condemned."

> "The unqualified are people just like me: broken, addicted, and lost. That is, until we encounter the magnificent love and transforming power of Christ. And it's in that moment of awakening that we realize God not only calls the unqualified to do His bidding in the earth, but He actually prefers them!"
>
> —Curvine Brewington, Christian hip-hop artist and evangelist, Dallas, TX

Now why would I share with you this flaw of mine? Because we avoid the noose of lost influence when we are honest about our hang-ups. I actually wrote about this issue in my life several years ago when I contributed a chapter called "The Death of a Salesman" to a book Dr. Bill Bright edited called *Living the Second-Mile Life*. When Dr. Bright asked me to write a chapter for his book, I knew I had to write about my lying issue. I have learned that when we are transparent about areas in which we have found freedom it will give others permission to get free. Writing that chapter helped me move past the failures of old and bring healing to others. I had leader after leader confide in me after reading that chapter that they too battled with honesty issues and were ready to be free. God takes what was meant to destroy us and uses it to transform us.

God wants to use the unqualified to confound the wise and "expose the hollow pretensions of the 'somebodies.'" Need I remind you of the key verse for this entire book? Here it is for you again:

> Take a good look, friends, at who you were when you got called into this life. I don't see many of "the brightest and the best" among you, not many influential, not many from high-society families. Isn't it obvious that God deliberately chose men and women that the culture overlooks and exploits and abuses, chose these "nobodies" to expose the hollow pretensions of the "somebodies"?
>
> —1 CORINTHIANS 1:26–28, THE MESSAGE

If this is the description of who God uses the most, then we have a lot working against us according to what man would say is success. That means we must be hungry to grow.

"The unqualified are the ones who lack the pedigree but maintain integrity. The ones who are missing education but pray for revelation. They aren't entertained with a title but will carry the towel."

—Jeremy White, youth pastor, Clermont, FL

Hungering After Growth

My goal with this chapter is to increase your hunger in eight different areas. That is why I've called this chapter "The Eight Insatiable Absolutes for the Unqualified." The word *insatiable* means "incapable of being satisfied or appeased."[2] I never want to be satisfied with where I am, and I hope you don't either. Life is too short to settle for a shallow existence. I want to be the one who will pull up to the buffet of God's table and "taste and see that the LORD is good!" (Ps. 34:8). God has called us to be hungry! Matthew 5:6 says, "You're blessed when you've worked up a good appetite for God. He's food and drink in the best meal you'll ever eat" (THE MESSAGE).

Are you hungry yet? I hear the dinner bell ringing!

- We must stay *hungry* for the Spirit.
- We must stay *hungry* for deep encounters with our King.
- We must stay *hungry* for biblical depth.
- We must stay *hungry* for knowledge.
- We must stay *hungry* for wisdom.
- We must stay *hungry* for personal growth.
- We must stay *hungry* for godly relationships.
- We must stay *hungry* for eternity in heaven.
- We must stay *hungry* for righteousness.

I don't want just an appetizer or some tiny portion on an overpriced menu—I want the smorgasbord! God's Word is like a Brazilian steak house, where you have to raise a flag on the table to stop the server from continuing to fill your plate with meat. The psalmist said it best:

> GOD, teach me lessons for living so I can stay the course. Give me insight so I can do what you tell me—my whole life one long, obedient response. Guide me

down the road of your commandments; I love traveling this freeway! Give me a bent for your words of wisdom, and not for piling up loot. Divert my eyes from toys and trinkets, invigorate me on the pilgrim way. Affirm your promises to me—promises made to all who fear you. Deflect the harsh words of my critics—but what you say is always so good. See how hungry I am for your counsel; preserve my life through your righteous ways!

—PSALM 119:33–40, THE MESSAGE

> "The unqualified know it's not the spotlight that makes them known. It's the time spent in the secret place that draws God's attention."
>
> —Joshua Vest, 25, ministry servant, Birmingham, AL

Rarely, if ever, do we have the opportunity to go back to the school of personal development when we reach a certain point in life. This is because life has the ability to drain us not only of time, but also the desire to grow personally. Maybe that's because when we arrive at certain places, we begin to give more than we receive. This can become dangerous to our foundation and future—which brings us right up to our first guideline. (By the way, if you decide to skip any of these foundational steps, you'll be in danger of tripping over your own statue dedicated in the honor of the lost heroes of a generation.)

Absolute #1: Encounter God More Than Man

God has called you to secret encounters and private glances. He created you for communion with Him first. When you neglect spending time with the Father, you will forget that you are His child. You'll allow your bond with God to break.

He will continually call out to you, reminding you that apart from Him, you are nothing.

> I am the Vine, you are the branches. When you're joined with me and I with you, the relation intimate and organic, the harvest is sure to be abundant. Separated, you can't produce a thing. Anyone who separates from me is deadwood, gathered up and thrown on the bonfire. But if you make yourselves at home with me and my words are at home in you, you can be sure that whatever you ask will be listened to and acted upon. This is how my Father shows who he is—when you produce grapes, when you mature as my disciples.
>
> —John 15:5–8, The Message

Absolute #2: Establish Early That You'll Be Blameless

What does *blameless* mean? In the Greek the word for blameless is *anegkletos*, and it means "unaccused, i.e. (by implication) irreproachable."[3] Your life will consist of mile markers that indicate where you have been, but you must never allow them to become your tombstone. The enemy would love for you to become a statistic rather than a statesman! Your future depends on it.

> The blameless spend their days under the Lord's care,
> and their inheritance will endure forever.
>
> —Psalm 37:18

If you will make up your mind to be unaccused, then the accuser of the brethren, Satan, will have to find someone else to bother. This means using wisdom in every aspect of your life. Avoid situations that could rob your integrity. Flat-out run from people who could steal your anointing. Make it your goal to never be a stumbling block for those who follow you. Your life is not your own! You belong to Jesus, your family, and the church. If you remain blameless, then when the accusations come—and I promise they will—you will be able to stand up with a clear conscience and say, "I am blameless! I have done no wrong."

I have made up my mind that I do not possess the right to embarrass the cross or disgrace my family. I want to be blessed!

> Blessed are those whose way is blameless, who walk in the law of the LORD.
>
> —PSALM 119:1, MEV

God has called us to be His image to the lost and not the devil's spokesperson for an undisciplined life. Lust will destroy those God planned to use, and it is not God's fault. As James tells us:

> Don't let anyone under pressure to give in to evil say, "God is trying to trip me up." God is impervious to evil, and puts evil in no one's way. The temptation to give in to evil comes from us and only us. We have no one to blame but the leering, seducing flare-up of our own lust. Lust gets pregnant, and has a baby: sin! Sin grows up to adulthood, and becomes a real killer.
>
> —JAMES 1:13–15, THE MESSAGE

My children deserve to be blessed and not embarrassed, because Proverbs 20:7 says, "The righteous lead blameless lives; blessed are their children after them." Look at the instruction of Paul to Titus, and notice the first thing he says:

> An elder must be blameless, faithful to his wife, a man whose children believe and are not open to the charge of being wild and disobedient. Since an overseer manages God's household, he must be blameless—not overbearing, not quick-tempered, not given to drunkenness, not violent, not pursuing dishonest gain. Rather, he must be hospitable, one who loves what is good, who is self-controlled, upright, holy and disciplined. He must hold firmly to the trustworthy message as it has been taught, so that he

can encourage others by sound doctrine and refute those who oppose it.
—Titus 1:6–9

The mouths of the naysayers will be shut when you are blameless. Your boldness will come forth like a lion.

Know this: God has anointed you for now. Don't waste it on a momentary lapse of stupidity. God wants to trust you with secrets, and that means you can have none. God is watching you (Ps. 101:6), and that's a good thing. It means you have God's attention.

Absolute #3: Establish Immovable Boundaries

On a similar note we must learn to draw a line in the sand and declare, "I refuse to cross that boundary." Some of the boundaries I established early on in my ministry are:

1. I will never look upon another woman with the wrong eyes.

2. I will never go any place that causes others to question the Jesus in me.

3. I will not partake in anything that could destroy my witness.

4. I will never harm those who have authority over my life.

5. I will do my best to guard my tongue so as to not harm others' reputations.

6. I will not joke in a manner that embarrasses the Holy Spirit.

7. I will love my family more than ministry, and I will love the church like Christ does.

8. I will honor my wife above myself.

9. I will be a man of my word.

> 10. I will stay in a place of brokenness before the Lord.

These boundaries have kept me pure for twenty-five years of ministry. I struggled with boundaries until I realized that they are there to protect my family and me. There is something inside of us all that hates boundaries. When it comes to sports, the referee will blow the whistle if you step out of bounds. Boundaries keep the game fair!

The unqualified must be people of boundaries. These are established limits that you have in your life that you refuse to cross. The Bible says God is the creator of boundaries (Ps. 74:17). The word for boundaries in the Hebrew is *gebulah*,[4] and it means "borders, landmarks, territories." In other words, it is the place you must stop. You need to establish places you stop—a place you say, "I can't cross that line!"

This is the place to develop your strength. The wall between you and death! This is not legalism but life rules. God has called the unqualified to be the ones who stand firm on biblical standards regardless of what wind of compromise comes your direction. Remember that 1 Corinthians 10:23 says everything is permissible but not everything is beneficial. This scripture declares you can do what you want, but that doesn't mean it is good for you.

> "I would rather be considered unqualified because it's the unqualified that God uses to do the unthinkable for His glory."
>
> —Sara Smiley, 22, ministry student, Tuscaloosa, AL

God has established laws for us in order to keep us from being thrown in a prison of pain. Proverbs 29:18 says, "Where there is no revelation, the people cast off restraint; but blessed is the one who heeds wisdom's instruction." The laws of God were established before you and me. The problem is that we now have a generation that thinks they can rewrite God's laws without consequences. To understand the boundaries of God, you must realize first that God has no limits and yet has established boundaries for us to live by.

Here are three simple boundaries that will keep your life in bounds:

1. Righteousness before the Lord

2. Justice in the eyes of the King

3. Fear of the Lord

God's very foundation is righteousness and justice (Ps. 89:14). *Righteousness* means "to stand right before God." You have be willing to remove anything from your life that could separate you from God. *Justice* means that regardless of what my flesh wants to do, I have decided to be upright and just before God.

> The LORD is exalted, for he dwells on high; he will fill Zion with his justice and righteousness. He will be the sure foundation for your times, a rich store of salvation and wisdom and knowledge; *the fear of the Lord is the key to this treasure.*
> —ISAIAH 33:5–6, EMPHASIS ADDED

When you have an awe of God and a holy fear of the Lord, it causes you to question your motives. If you will choose to live a life of righteousness, abound in justice, and walk in the fear of the Lord at all times, you will have a life of victory. Remember that the beginning of wisdom is the fear of the Lord (Prov. 9:10).

The cross of Jesus establishes our boundaries! Jesus said in Luke 14:27, "And whoever who does not carry their cross and follow me cannot be my disciple." It will be very hard to wander into the wrong land while carrying the cross. Why?

Because the destination of the cross is a hill where you die to self.

> "The unqualified is the application torn up and thrown in the trash, the last kid picked on the playground, the teen that can't lose enough weight or find a date. To invest into the life of the unqualified is to feel the very heartbeat of Jesus."
>
> —Wes Brinson, student pastor, Raleigh, NC

Freedom of the flesh is actually the chain that binds us. Paul said it best in Galatians, when he warned against the wrong freedom and not living by the Spirit:

> You, brothers, have been called to liberty. Only do not use liberty to give an opportunity to the flesh, but by love serve one another. For the entire law is fulfilled in one word, even in this: "You shall love your neighbor as yourself." But if you bite and devour one another, take heed that you are not consumed by one another. I say then, walk in the Spirit, and you shall not fulfill the lust of the flesh. For the flesh lusts against the Spirit, and the Spirit against the flesh. These are in opposition to one another, so that you may not do the things that you please. But if you are led by the Spirit, you are not under the law. Now the works of the flesh are revealed, which are these: adultery, sexual immorality, impurity, lewdness, idolatry, sorcery, hatred, strife, jealousy, rage, selfishness, dissensions, heresies, envy, murders, drunkenness, carousing, and the like. I warn you, as I previously warned you, that those who do such things shall not inherit the kingdom of God. But the fruit of the Spirit is love, joy, peace, patience, gentleness, goodness, faith, meekness, and self-control; against such there is no law. Those who are Christ's

> have crucified the flesh with its passions and lusts. If we live in the Spirit, let us also walk in the Spirit.
> —GALATIANS 5:13–25, MEV

I challenge you to create boundaries to live by. They will protect you!

Absolute #4: Work Hard and Remain Teachable

Show me any great achiever, whether in ministry, business, sports, medicine, or academics, and I will show you somebody who worked to become who they are today. It doesn't just happen.

I often see young leaders who have bought into the mindset that charisma and gifts are the key qualities to success. Those things are on the surface, but true longevity comes from a life of consecration. I have often heard it said, "Never allow your gifts to take you where your character cannot keep you." The true test of a great leader is what comes out of his cup when it gets bumped. We must have God at our very core.

Guard against laziness and slothfulness. You have to be willing to carry the load an extra mile, as Jesus said in Matthew 5:41: "If a soldier demands that you carry his gear for a mile, carry it two miles" (NLT). What? Why do I have to do that? That is exactly what the underachiever would ask. In a day where entitlement from every direction is creating a "gimme" generation, we must be the ones who will show up early and leave late. That is a true sign of a servant heart.

If you choose to live a life that just gets by and you refuse to work hard, then you will end up having a master named poverty. Don't believe me? Look at what Proverbs has to say:

> You lazy fool, look at an ant. Watch it closely; let it teach you a thing or two. Nobody has to tell it what to do. All summer it stores up food; at harvest it stockpiles provisions. So how long are you going to laze

around doing nothing? How long before you get out of bed? A nap here, a nap there, a day off here, a day off there, sit back, take it easy—do you know what comes next? Just this: You can look forward to a dirt-poor life, poverty your permanent houseguest!

—PROVERBS 6:6–11, THE MESSAGE

A teachable spirit must accompany the work-hard mentality. You will never know everything on your own. This means you have to be willing to study and learn past your own intellect. Show me a person who is teachable, and I will show you someone who scares the enemy. I can promise I have never been the smartest in the room, but few can match my insatiable thirst for knowledge—and I hope my life keeps the devil on his toes!

Study to show yourself approved by God, a workman who need not be ashamed, rightly dividing the word of truth.

—2 TIMOTHY 2:15, MEV

The New International Version puts it this way:

Do your best to present yourself to God as one approved, a worker who does not need to be ashamed and who correctly handles the word of truth.

Absolute #5: Stay Focused on the Prize

First Corinthians 9:24 says, "Do you not know that in a race all the runners run, but only one gets the prize? Run in such a way as to get the prize." You must stay focused on the prize. This is critical if you are to be faithful to the call of God that is on your life. So many distractions can stop you from finishing the race for God.

So, what is the prize? It's hearing the words "Well done." Jesus tells us to hold on because there is a reward coming (Matt. 25:21).

The calling of God will keep you focused in good times or

bad times. You can't suddenly decide to take off your mantle because you're ready to quit. Romans 11:29 tells us, "God's gifts and God's call are under full warranty—never canceled, never rescinded" (THE MESSAGE). In life and ministry, what is said of our life at the end is what matters. My prayer for you is that your eulogy will end with, "He/she was faithful till the end!"

People often go into ministry with wrong motives and impure concepts. I have seen many line up at the running blocks and fire off great, but they stumble along the way. The apostle Paul wrapped up his life with these words in 2 Timothy 4:7: "I have fought the good fight, I have finished the race, I have kept the faith." Furthermore, God will give you everything you need to finish: "And God is able to bless you abundantly, so that in all things at all times, having all that you need, you will abound in every good work" (2 Cor. 9:8). There is no excuse. You cannot quit on the One who would not quit on you. There is a prize waiting!

> "The unqualified would rather hear, 'Well done, faithful son,' than obtain the system's position of favorite son!"
> —Carey Harrell, pastor, Roanoke, VA

Absolute #6: Understand Spiritual Authority

God will never elevate you past the place you stopped honoring those who are in a position of authority over you. This doesn't mean you have to always agree with the leaders' actions, but it does mean you understand God is the One who establishes their authority.

> Let every person be subject to the governing authorities, for there is no authority except from God, and those that exist are appointed by God. Therefore

> whoever resists the authority resists what God has
> appointed, and those who resist will incur judgment.
> Rulers are not a terror to good works, but to evil works.
> Do you wish to have no fear of the authority? Do what
> is good, and you will have praise from him, for he is
> the servant of God for your good. But if you do what
> is evil, be afraid, for he does not bear the sword in
> vain, for he is the servant of God, an avenger to exe-
> cute wrath upon him who practices evil. So it is nec-
> essary to be in subjection, not only because of wrath,
> but also for the sake of conscience.
>   —ROMANS 13:1–5, MEV

You and I will never become who we are called to be if
we do not have someone mentoring us who can take us to
another level. This is not always easy to do. We must understand that, since the beginning of our lives, self-preservation
has been driven into our psyche. The natural reaction to
authority is rebellion. God places us under authority so we
can learn to die to our flesh. True disciples must kill their
flesh daily in order to resurrect their spirits.

I believe that true spiritual authority is never activated
over our lives until we are in a position to rebel. There is no
perfect leader, but they are in your life for your good. Paul
said it this way: "For the one in authority is God's servant for
your good. But if you do wrong, be afraid, for rulers do not
bear the sword for no reason. They are God's servants, agents
of wrath to bring punishment on the wrongdoer" (Rom. 13:4).
If you will learn to walk under a covering and not rebel, God
will raise you up to lead. Recognizing those over you will
bring recognition of what God has done in you!

I understand there are times when we might be forced to
work under a leader who is abusive. This can either destroy
you or make you stronger. When you are forced to submit to
a leader who crosses the boundaries of effective and trusted
leadership, oftentimes that is when you will have to decide

whether God wants you to stay or leave. I truly believe that if you can see the person's flaws then so can everyone else.

> "The unqualified live in the very real tension of being responsible to others to have answers, vision, leadership, and authority yet knowing they are desperately in need of God's supply of each of them. They are keenly aware of their inabilities and yet have still answered, 'Here am I, Lord, send me!'"
>
> —Travis Jenkins, pastor, Oklahoma City, OK

Many years ago I accepted a position as a youth pastor at a very large church. I was at the church for only three months. Upon accepting the position, Karen and I quickly realized that we had made the wrong decision. The pastor I worked for was a good man, but very flawed in his leadership style and approach to people. During this season I learned the power of prayer and brokenness. The pastor was harsh and uncouth in the pulpit. He often berated the people from the pulpit and dismissed his staff's concerns. I honestly believe he had serious mental problems.

The church was an absolute mess, and soon the board and congregation took matters into their own hands and removed the pastor. Once the pastor was removed, we also left the church for a new location. I share this because there were times when I knew the board was holding a secret meeting about the pastor, and I felt so conflicted. I knew I should tell my pastor, but I also knew that the people's concerns were valid. I eventually told the pastor of the meetings I knew had taken place, but things only got worse. I would leave the office to go home each day and oftentimes find myself driving with tears rolling down my face. I would cry out to God to deliver us from that place.

It was during that time that I read a very powerful book

called *A Tale of Three Kings* by Gene Edwards. This book transformed my life. It speaks of the struggles David experienced while dealing with King Saul. This book taught me how to understand true brokenness and how to guard against bitterness. I can remember lying on my living room floor weeping as I read that book. Here is a powerful quote from the book:

> David was caught in a very uncomfortable position; however, he seemed to grasp a deep understanding of the unfolding drama in which he had been caught. He seemed to understand something that few of even the wisest men of his day understood. Something that in our day, when men are wiser still, even fewer understand. And what was that? God did not have—but wanted very much to have—men and women who would live in pain. God wanted a broken vessel.[5]

It took me years to understand why we had to go through that dark time. I can look back and realize that I learned some very important lessons. The greatest lesson I learned was that submission is a theory until it costs you something. When you're working under an abusive leader, God will either give you the grace to endure or the will to walk away and start anew.

Always use these three guidelines when determining whether or not you should stay under a difficult leader:

1. Choose to learn from this season. It will teach you more than you can imagine. Trust God, and He will deliver you. While determining whether to stay or leave, remain faithful where you are and to whom you are serving. If you do, God will elevate you in no time. When you are faithful, God will someday give you the proper spiritual authority.

2. Evaluate the risks. Determine whether you or your family are in danger. If so, then you must leave.

3. Seek God. Ask yourself, "Has God released me to go into another direction?" God will speak! Listen for His voice! Whatever you do, don't abandon your call because of a bad leader.

Spiritual authority is not removed when the disciple surpasses the leader but when it is handed to someone else. There will be a battle when authority comes in conflict with self-preservation. You must allow God to fight your battles. Remember, God exalts the humble (Matt. 23:12). I truly believe that the next level of ministry is always determined by the foundation of the earlier times of submission.

Remember these twelve rules when it comes to working for a leader that God has put in place over your life:

1. The anointing on the leader that you now serve was birthed in the tough seasons (Ps. 119:89).

2. The way you treat the leader who is over you will determine how those under you will later treat you (1 Pet. 3:9).

3. Until you stand in a leader's shoes, you will never understand the battles they fight. Use this season to grow and learn wisdom (Prov. 2:6–8).

4. God trusts you to honor your leader regardless of their disposition (1 Thess. 5:12–13).

5. The closer you get to a leader, the more you will be able to see the flaws in their armor (Eph. 6:13–18).

6. Learn from your leader during this season, and God will use it in your future to transform lives (Prov. 3:5–6).

7. Honor the good you can see in your leader, ask God to give you the grace to handle their humanity, and trust God to handle them (Prov. 25:4–5).

8. Let your life be a reminder to your leader that God always exalts the humble (1 Pet. 3:8–12).

9. Guard your heart at all times so that bitterness doesn't poison the well of your ministry (Prov. 4:23–26).

10. Remember that you are being refined and that the day will come when you will be released to your next season (Isa. 48:10).

11. Remember too that those who are called must have an attitude of gratitude. Thankfulness is a sign you didn't do it on your own (Heb. 12:28–29).

12. Always remember where you came from. You didn't just arrive; people helped you. People believed in you, and people sacrificed for you. You're not an overnight success but rather a God project (Eph. 2:4–6).

> "The unqualified are the ones the world has put on the sidelines, but God will use their scars; He'll use them to change the game."
>
> —David Schlueter, youth pastor, Peoria, AZ

Absolute #7: Know That "Suddenly" Is Never Sudden

I want you to live in a place of miracles, and God does too. The thing is, when it comes to miracles, God is never shocked by what happens. He is never blown away. He is all-knowing! I believe God is calling us all to the suddenly, but we must also realize there is no such thing as a sudden suddenly. What do I mean? Any "suddenly" we encounter is always the result of a long process.

I am always amazed at how shocked we are when God does what He has promised. I am even more shocked when we do not realize it was the end result of a lot of actions that led to a door of opportunity. When you are willing to live out the absolutes mentioned in this chapter, then you will experience the suddenly!

In Acts 2:2 we read, "Suddenly a sound like the blowing of a violent wind came from heaven and filled the whole house where they were sitting." This may have seemed like a sudden occurrence, but remember the disciples had been waiting in the Upper Room for ten days. (And that's not to mention the thousands of years of activity and expectation that led to that moment too!)

I can certainly relate to the "suddenly" that's preceded by so much waiting. When I was seventeen years old, I dreamed of a building packed with thousands of worshippers crying out to God. Then I walked to the stage and began to speak. I awoke thinking this would happen very soon. It didn't! It wasn't until twenty years later, while preaching in Australia, that I walked to the platform to speak and suddenly realized the dream from twenty years earlier was being fulfilled. I wasn't ready at seventeen; I was barely ready at thirty-seven! The "suddenly" is the realization of a catalyst moment that comes when you simply walked out God's promise and did the simple things faithfully.

We must be careful here because there are times we would love to rush the process. We cry out! We stomp our feet and often get discouraged, and God waits until we are done to show us His timing. If you are not willing to work hard and wait on the process, you will be in a heap of trouble.

> Better to be ordinary and work for a living than act
> important and starve in the process.
> —PROVERBS 12:9, THE MESSAGE

There is always a process! Wait on the timing of the Lord. When it comes to the things of God, we must be patient and always allow the process to work itself out. It is in the process that we grow the greatest. If God actually gave you what you wanted right now, then you probably wouldn't be ready. The equation of suddenly looks like this:

> Personal awakening + revelation + obedience + discipline + planning = suddenly

For years I had faith in what God was planning to do in our lives, but as I got older I developed trust. God will always take you from faith to trust—and faith and trust are on two completely different levels!

> "To be called unqualified is a compliment. It means we are free to create, adapt, and innovate without the religious bonds of man-made traditions. We are true to God's truth and determined to accomplish His mission."
>
> —Alex Pratt, youth pastor, West Monroe, LA

Faith is what happens when I join my heart with God's and believe for something great. Hebrews 4:14 says, "Therefore, since we have a great high priest who has ascended into heaven, Jesus the Son of God, let us hold firmly to the faith we profess." And 2 Corinthians 5:7 says, "For we walk by faith, not by sight" (MEV). This is level one.

Once you develop faith, you eventually move to the next level: trust. Trust is what happens when you not only believe something will happen, but you also move forward without doubting that God has it. Trust is knowing God sees right where you are and hasn't forgotten you.

> Trust in the LORD with all your heart, and lean not on your own understanding; in all your ways acknowledge Him, and He will direct your paths.
> —PROVERBS 3:5–6, MEV

There will be times when the "suddenly" seems so far away. It will be so easy to feel discouraged and defeated. The suddenly will come; you just have to hold on. It costs to have a suddenly! This is what separates the finishers from starters. Throughout the Bible every "suddenly" took place because of a process. There are no shortcuts. Will you see the miracle or hear someone else's story?

> "Unqualified is the label that many have put me under. I've come to this conclusion. The anointing in you and on you is greater than the ability and talents that man wants you to measure up to. We must realize that the no of the doubter was canceled out by the resounding yes of the Father."
>
> —Drew Craig, worship and youth pastor, Billings, MO

When you get tired waiting for your suddenly, imagine the end result in order to push past your present pain. There is glory just around the corner! God's promise is that restoration will come your direction (Joel 2:25–26).

The unqualified will only be able to live at a place of expectancy when they allow God to be their protector, provider, and point of no return. God hasn't forgotten you, but during this time the world might. God is bringing it all together!

Shall I bring to the point of birth and not cause delivery? says the LORD. Shall I who cause delivery shut the womb? says your God.

—ISAIAH 66:9, MEV

Five Essential Attitudes for the "Suddenly"

- Be tuned in. God speaks when we least expect it. Matthew 3:17 says, "And a voice came from heaven, saying, "This is My beloved Son, in whom I am well pleased" (MEV).

- Be vigilant. We have to respond to the storms of life when we least expect them. Don't react, but act upon them. Be ready for the attack. First Peter 5:8 says, "Be sober and watchful, because your adversary the devil walks around as a roaring lion, seeking whom he may devour" (MEV).

- Be prepared. The master will require an account of our lives when we least expect it. Mark 13:36 says, "If he comes suddenly, do not let him find you sleeping."

- Be ready. There will be demands on our anointing, and miracles will happen when you least expect them. Matthew 9:20 says, "Then a woman, who was ill with a flow of blood for twelve years, came behind Him and touched the hem of His garment" (MEV).

- Be expectant. Encounters with God will happen when we least expect them. Do your homework, and you can handle the pop quiz. Acts 1:10–11 says, "While they looked intently toward heaven as He ascended, suddenly two men stood by them in white garments. They said, "Men of Galilee, why stand looking toward heaven? This same Jesus, who was taken up from you to heaven, will come in like manner as you saw Him go into heaven" (MEV).

Absolute #8: Build an Ark

I have often seen the unqualified struggle in the area of finances, and maybe you can relate to this. Many times the weight of finances can stand in the way of dreaming a big dream for God. I believe that if the unqualified do not understand the principles of God's kingdom in the area of finances, they will never achieve their goals.

We know that God is not short on money and that He "has pleasure in the prosperity of His servant" (Ps. 35:27, NKJV). We are promised that finances will come to the righteous (Prov. 13:21–22). Jesus also told us that we are to seek Him first (Matt. 6:33).

> "The unqualified is often the most unexpected to be used when God assigns people for His tasks. Think about Peter, Paul, and Mary. Peter needed a career change, Paul needed a life-change event, and Mary an immaculate conception. Talk about God thinking and acting outside the box!"
>
> —Bruce Donisthorpe, business leader, Albuquerque, NM

We learn from all this that when your priorities are in order, God will take care of the rest. He will give it to you if He knows that it won't own you.

> Honor the LORD with your wealth, with the firstfruits of all your crops; then your barns will be filled to over-flowing, and your vats will brim over with new wine.
> —PROVERBS 3:9–10

Your firstfruits, which is your tithe, belong to the Lord. I challenge you to be a giver. Learn the power of sowing and reaping. Jesus made another promise in Luke 6:38: "Give, and it will be given to you. A good measure, pressed down, shaken together and running over, will be poured into your lap. For with the measure you use, it will be measured to you." God knows how to measure your obedience.

Often those who are going into ministry are not willing to ask God how to make a living out in the world. God will give you an entrepreneurial anointing that will not only bless your family but also the kingdom of God.

This powerful scripture in Hebrews 11:6–7 changed my life on this subject:

> And without faith it is impossible to please God, for he who comes to God must believe that He exists and that He is a rewarder of those who diligently seek Him. By faith Noah, being divinely warned about things not yet seen, moved with godly fear, prepared an ark to save his family, by which he condemned the world and became an heir of the righteousness that comes by faith.
>
> —MEV

I had read verse 6 many times—that "without faith it is impossible to please God"—but I had never taken notice of verse 7. It says, "By faith Noah, being divinely warned about things not yet seen, moved with godly fear, prepared an ark to save his family." This scripture ignited me, because so often we fail to plan for our future. Noah built an ark! Noah had no idea how to prepare for the storm. He had never seen a boat, but God gave him the plan. I am not just talking about finances here because finances alone will not fill the voids in your life.

God wants to give you a plan. He will anoint you with ideas and dreams to build an ark for your family. The Bible says that when you are godly, the finances will be in the house!

> Blessed is the man who fears the LORD, who delights greatly in His commandments. His offspring shall be

mighty in the land; the generation of the upright shall be blessed. Wealth and riches shall be in his house, and his righteousness endures forever.

—Psalm 112:1–3, mev

I challenge you to ask God for ideas to finance your dreams. I have many friends to whom God has given dreams, visions, or prophetic words that gave them ideas to create wealth. God will give you the idea, so always keep a pen and paper with you. You never know when inspiration will come from the Holy Spirit. I truly believe that as our nation continues to decline economically, God is going to use His people to bring forth blessings. Ecclesiastes 11:1–2 says, "Cast your bread upon the waters, for you will find it after many days. Give a portion to seven, or even eight, for you do not know what calamity may happen on the earth" (mev). *Cast your bread*—in other words, sow seeds for your future!

The Bible Is Full of Entrepreneurs

- Noah owned the first boat.
- Isaac re-dug the ancient wells.
- Jacob had a dream of speckled and spotted sheep—that, by the way, was after he promised to pay tithe.
- Joseph cornered the market on grain commodities.
- David killed a giant.
- Peter owned a fishing business.
- Paul made tents.
- Jesus had a fish-and-biscuit business!

Here is where you begin: plan, dream, become responsible, pay your tithe, get over your past financial mistakes, clean up any bad credit, cry out to God for wisdom, seek out direction, and get in His Word. You must develop lifestyle patterns that will positively affect your future and give you room to work hard.

> "The unqualified is being outside the collective group with talent and natural giftings. It is the 'not even considered' option because of previous tendencies or even past actions. It is the 'one in a million' success story that could only have been accomplished by something greater than oneself. I want to be unqualified so anything that is accomplished reflects God."
>
> —Jeff Martin, high school teacher, entrepreneur, and lay pastor, Demotte, IN

Remember, this is number eight of the "Insatiable Absolutes of the Unqualified"—and the number eight means new beginnings!

> "I'm unqualified! I don't have a PhD. I come from a divorced home. Statistics said I shouldn't have made it. But now I'm blessed, I'm married, and I'm living my life for God's glory! The unqualified is the song of my life!"
>
> —Quinton Carter, youth pastor, Houston, TX

As I close this chapter, my prayer is that you will establish these eight insatiable absolutes. Heaven is looking for those who will stand tall with the King. On that note I'll share with you one of my favorite quotes from C. S. Lewis:

> For He seems to do nothing of Himself which He can possibly delegate to His creatures. He commands us to do slowly and blunderingly what He could do perfectly and in the twinkling of an eye. He allows

us to neglect what He would have us do, or to fail. Perhaps we do not fully realize the problem, so to call it, of enabling finite free wills to co-exist with Omnipotence. It seems to involve at every moment almost a sort of divine abdication. We are not mere recipients or spectators. We are either privileged to share in the game or compelled to collaborate in the work, "to wield our little tridents." Is this amazing process simply Creation going on before our eyes?[6]

Stay hungry, my friends!

Chapter 10

YOU CAN'T CUT MY HAIR!

> "Realizing that you are unqualified brings freedom because your motivation is no longer about self-promotion and self-gratification but rather about making known the One who qualifies and gives your life purpose!"
>
> —Karen Schatzline, evangelist and author, Birmingham, AL

THE HAIR OF the Samson church is growing back."
Those are words I once heard Pastor Glen Berteau declare in a powerful service as people ran to the altar for an encounter. And as we will see in this chapter, that's exactly what we need to see happen in the church.

Who was Samson? He's one of the most well-known persons in the Bible, mainly for the hair on his head that made him so strong. As a child, my brother Scott and I would wrestle and declare, "I am Samson!" He was cool. In our minds he was a crazy WWF/WWE wrestler like the great Hacksaw Jim Duggan! I imagined him marching around flexing his muscles, challenging any and all to a fight. Little did I know that someday I would write a chapter in a book about the life of this very tarnished judge of Israel.

Everyone loves the account of Samson. It has suspense, fight scenes, romance, broken hearts, pain, and victory at the end. In fact, Hollywood has made movies and cartoons that usually depict a He-Man version of Samson who had a fatal flaw called lust, when in reality there is so much more to the story.

The Place of Discipline

One day while I was praying, the Lord spoke to me, saying, "Son, don't let the enemy cut your hair!" I knew exactly what God was saying to me. As I prayed, I said, "Lord, I promise to do my very best to watch for the Delilahs that could come into my life." God said to me, "Delilah was the end result of a life of no discipline."

Discipline is proof that God is a good father. The Bible tells us discipline is the key component to becoming a usable vessel for the Lord. We are orphans in search of a father when we have no discipline in our lives.

> In your struggle against sin, you have not yet resisted to the point of shedding your blood. And have you completely forgotten this word of encouragement that addresses you as a father addresses his son? It says, "My son, do not make light of the Lord's discipline, and do not lose heart when he rebukes you, because the Lord disciplines the one he loves, and he chastens everyone he accepts as his son." Endure hardship as discipline; God is treating you as His children. For what children are not disciplined by their father? If you are not disciplined—and everyone undergoes discipline—then you are not legitimate, not true sons and daughters at all. Moreover, we have all had human fathers who disciplined us and we respected them for it. How much more should we submit to the Father of spirits and live! They disciplined us for a little while as they thought best; but God disciplines us for our good, in order that we may share in his holiness. No discipline seems pleasant at the time, but painful. Later on,

however, it produces a harvest of righteousness and
peace for those who have been trained by it.
                                        —Hebrews 12:4–11

We are living in a day when the very thought of disci-
plining a child is contrary to culture. Households are often
ruled by community consensus rather than the parents who
are engaged in rearing the child. Along with this view of
child rearing, it seems now we view God as an uncle rather
than a father. An uncle usually shows up when it's conve-
nient, but a father is there at all times. Without fathers in
our lives, we will always search for our identity.

God is a good father who desires only to see you mature
into His original plan for your life. He wants to trust you
with big things, but the little things you are called to conquer will conquer you when you refuse to submit to discipline. We have all heard, "It's the little foxes that spoil the
vine." That is actually taken from Song of Solomon 2:15. It
means the little things in your life can affect your harvest.
The small, undisciplined areas of your life will make you a
casualty of your own flesh-screaming bacteria called the self.

"God in His wisdom has historically chosen unqualified
people to shape world history—people who are qualified
by grace and empowered by love because they said yes
to God."

—Tom Crandall, youth pastor, Bethel
Church, Redding, CA

The greatest hindrance to the call of God is our flesh.
I have often said, "I would rather be an unknown person
of faith than a well-known person of lost influence." The
moment you were born, the enemy set his sights on you. His
goal is to wear you out in such a way that the fight will dis-
appear from your spirit. That is why we must look at the life

of a judge named Samson and learn what we can from him in this area.

Honor Your Vows

Samson was born at a time when Israel was under judgment from God for forty years because of sin (Judg. 13:1). God had placed the Philistines over them to rule them, and Samson was meant to be a gift from God to the people of Israel. He was supposed to be the one who would deliver the people out of the hands of the Philistines.

The Bible says his very birth was miraculous. Samson's parents could not have children, and an angel came to visit his mother:

> The angel of the LORD appeared to her and said, "You are barren and childless, but you are going to become pregnant and give birth to a son. Now see to it that you drink no wine or other fermented drink and that you do not eat anything unclean. You will become pregnant and have a son whose head is never to be touched by a razor because the boy is to be a Nazirite, dedicated to God from the womb. He will take the lead in delivering Israel from the hands of the Philistines."
> —JUDGES 13:3–5

The thing that's interesting to note here is that God has no trouble making promises to us that come with conditions. God tells Samson's mom that her son will someday take the lead in delivering Israel—that is, if he will keep his Nazirite vow.

The term *Nazirite* means "consecrated or holy unto Yahweh." As Samson was a Nazirite, Samson's mother was given three guidelines for raising him that she would also be required to keep. Not ten, not twenty-five, just three:

1. Do not give him wine.

2. Do not cut his hair.

3. Do not let him go near anything dead.

We know Samson kept his vows when he was a child because the Bible says, "The boy grew, and the LORD blessed him. The Spirit of the LORD began to move upon him" (Judg. 13:24–25, MEV). God was preparing him for greatness. He was the great hope of Israel. All he had to do was honor the vows!

> "The unqualified are those who have been called but rejected, useful but broken, redeemed but emptied, powerful but humbled, anointed but hidden. These men and women are the righteous remnant about their Father's business, revealing the kingdom of God on the earth today!"
> —Deon Lett, apostle and pastor, Saint Petersburg, FL

Desires Lead to a Fall

Many times we want the anointing and the stage without the intrusion of conviction from the Holy Spirit. God loves you enough to give you rules. He will give you precepts that lead to freedom from a life of destruction.

It was the same way in the Garden of Eden, where God told Adam and Eve they could enjoy the entire garden, but oh, by the way, stay away from that one tree; it is forbidden. When God establishes His anointing on our lives, our success is determined by our obedience. Obedience often requires death. We know that one man's disobedience under a tree eventually led to one Man's obedience upon a tree. (See Romans 5:19.)

When God looks at you and me, He sees a partnership,

not a one-man show. God joins with our faith, and the end result can be supernatural. Yet when we begin to believe we have arrived here on our own, God steps back and watches the death of potential. The more confident we become in ourselves, the less God can use us. If the stage has the power to seduce you, God will always be required to reduce you! God never asked us to be shooting stars but people who chase the star like the wise men who searched for Jesus. God never asked you to build your kingdom but His! As John the Baptist said, "He must increase, but I must decrease!" (John 3:30, NAS).

> "Acknowledging that you're unqualified means that you will have to acknowledge that you are not the cause of success."
>
> —Nate Schatzline, youth pastor, The House, Modesto, CA

I must make a plea here, then, to all of the unqualified who are preparing to be used of God in an extraordinary way. Please die! Die to your flesh. Die to your preconceived concepts of fame. Die to desiring to see your name in lights. We must work out our own salvation at the altar of desperation. The apostle Paul gave us great instruction when he wrote in Philippians 2:12–15:

> Therefore, my beloved, as you have always obeyed, not only in my presence, but so much more in my absence, work out your own salvation with fear and trembling. For God is the One working in you, both to will and to do His good pleasure. Do all things without murmuring and disputing, that you may be blameless and harmless, sons of God, without fault, in the midst of a crooked and perverse generation, in which you shine as lights in the world.
>
> —MEV

We will never shine so bright as when the humiliation of self has taken place on the platform of brokenness. It is when we humble ourselves and cry out to God that He walks into the room like a father embracing a child during a storm.

Get back to the prayer closet! The scariest place you will ever visit is the dusty and cobwebbed room of an abandoned prayer life. It is a scary place because you're all alone. You have to deal with you when you are all alone, and that is not easy when it is you who needs to change. God has the ability to force you into the place of self-confrontation. I have often said, "The end of self is the beginning of God!" It is when we wander into the deserted prayer closet that God turns it into the holy of holies.

Leonard Ravenhill once said, "The self-satisfied don't need to pray. The self-sufficient don't want to pray. The self-righteous cannot pray. But the man who realizes, 'I need something outside of anything that's human at all,' he wants to bathe his soul in prayer."[1] No matter how gifted we are or how beloved by the crowds, eventually night comes down upon us all, and the silence of closed heavens screams loudly. The vacuum we often feel in our spirits is not a vacuum of unopened doors, but a vacuum of God's jealousy for His bride. God is calling for His bride to come to Him.

Revelation 4:1 says, "After this I looked, and there before me was a door standing open in heaven. And the voice I had first heard speaking to me like a trumpet said, 'Come up here, and I will show you what must take place after this.'" God has not called you to walk the bride down the aisle. That is God's role. Many times we are on the wrong arm! God is the groom at the wedding. The safest place you will ever be is in the presence of a Savior who knows the real you!

Don't Ignore the Flaws

Samson rode to prominence among the people of Israel. Everywhere he went, he represented God's covenant with

His wayward children. As long as Samson was around, they knew God still had a plan. The people of Israel were willing to overlook Samson's character flaws because their personal deliverance was more important than the integrity of the leader they were following.

This sounds like what we're experiencing in America. Too often we are willing to put our morals on the shelf of yesterday's ideals and embrace any ideology regardless of the lie. We are quick to hitch our bandwagon to someone with lofty words and empty promises, just as long as our self-preservation and bank accounts grow. When that doesn't happen or can't happen because the foundation of the individual is too shallow, we then blame the system and not the man or ourselves. Americans elected a president to lead them regardless of the fact that as a state senator he voted against the Born Alive Infant Protection Act *four* times, which would have protected babies who survived abortion. Instead he voted in favor of leaving them to die.[2] Now America is enjoying his promise of hope and change as we watch the morals of our nation slide into oblivion.

> "God takes the unqualified and gives them a platform of significance to show how big God is!"
> —Shaun Koch, youth and associate pastor, Colombo, Sri Lanka

The life of Samson can teach us a lot about the dangers of not following God's mandates. Let's review a timeline of Samson's life:

- In Judges 14 he wants to marry a Philistine woman. On the way he kills a lion, but later he comes back to the lion and finds a beehive in its belly. He pulls the honey from the dead animal and feeds his parents (breaking the condition of never touching a dead thing). He goes to marry the woman. While at the marriage feast he shares a riddle about the honey he pulled from the lion. His wife pesters him until he reveals the riddle, and when the Philistines know the answer, Samson gets mad and kills thirty Philistines, and his wife is given to another man.

- In Judges 15:3–4 Samson tries to visit his wife and realizes that she has been given to another man. He gets so mad at the Philistines that he torches the tails of three hundred foxes, and as they run they burn up the Philistines' fields.

- In Judges 15:6 the Philistines retaliate against Samson by killing the woman Samson had married along with her father. Then in Judges 15:15 Samson kills a thousand Philistines with the jawbone of a donkey (again, Samson touched something that was dead).

- In Judges 15:18–19 God provides water miraculously to a thirsty Samson from a hole in the ground.

- In Judges 15:20 we read that Samson led Israel for twenty years in the days of the Philistines. Then in Judges 16:1–3 Samson visits a prostitute and gets ambushed by the Philistines. He responds by ripping the gates off the city.

- In Judges 16:4 Samson meets Delilah.

What does this timeline show us? We will give an account when we are not accountable! Let me explain.

Somewhere along the way Samson forgot that His mission from God wasn't about Him but about a people who needed to be delivered. His life began to take a horrible turn when he felt he could live like the enemy. Yes, he was anointed but he wasn't disciplined. He forgot his covenant. I believe that began the day he pulled honey from the lion he had killed (Judg. 14:6). He saw a beehive in the belly of the dead lion, and he took the honey.

The Bible says in Judges 14:9, "He scooped out the honey with his hands and ate as he went along. When he rejoined his parents, he gave them some, and they too ate it. But he did not tell them that he had taken the honey from the lion's carcass." Why didn't his mother ask him where he got the honey? Did she forget the commandment the angel gave her in Judges 13 that her son was to take a Nazarite vow? As part of that vow, Samson couldn't even go near something that had been dead for a while, much less touch it and eat something from its belly. Samson had tricked his family into breaking the law of God, and they didn't even know it. Where was his accountability? We must be willing to ask questions of those whom God has entrusted His authority to. In his disobedience Samson led his own family astray.

We must make ourselves accountable to the voices of wisdom God puts in our lives. The moment we turn our ears away from God's voice, or the voice of our spouses and our shepherds, then we begin a slow demise. The root of most failure is usually heartache, pain, and disappointment that was never healed. It will show up again in our lives, and often when it does we reproduce in others our pain. We must understand the heart of the Father for His children. When we wander down a road of compromise, inevitably we eventually leave victims in our wake.

Your family deserves the best you that you can be. I am reminded of something I heard Pastor Zane Anderson from Victory Worship Center, Tucson, Arizona, say last year. He said, "Your destiny does not trump your stupidity. You are anointed, but you can't expect your choices not to impact your calling!" We are living in a time when many people seem to think human effort in ministry is more important than God-empowered leadership. Jesus said in John 14:12, "Very truly I tell you, whoever believes in me will do the works I have been doing, and they will do even greater things than these, because I am going to the Father." God doesn't need you to be a substitute teacher for Him. He simply needs you to get out of the way and let Him move among His people. If we ever begin to think of the ministry as a job, then we will begin to desire a payday. When the gospel becomes our job, we have gone from good news to bad press!

We are in this battle together, but how can we be a winning army if we refuse to do war together. We need one another. We are not in competition. I often hear ministers speak of other ministers or churches as if they are in competition. It is dangerous to compete with those we are called to run with. It seems we have forgotten what we are supposed to be in battle against. The enemy loves it when we set our sights on one another and miss the real mark, which is the enemy. Ephesians 6:12 says, "For our struggle is not against flesh and blood, but against the rulers, against the authorities, against the powers of this dark world and against the spiritual forces of evil in the heavenly realms."

When you are more concerned about performance than God's presence, you will allow yourself to be ruled by whatever the "relevant factor" seems to be. When this happens, the crowd determines the depths into which we go in God and that is, most often, very shallow territory. The relevant factor is what is forcing the unqualified to arise! First Corinthians 3:18–20 says, "Don't fool yourself. Don't think that you can be wise merely by being up-to-date with the times. Be God's fool—that's the path to true wisdom. What the world calls smart, God calls stupid. It's written in Scripture, He exposes the chicanery of the chic. The Master sees through the smoke screens of the know-it-alls" (The Message). I often wonder how many times we are having so much fun playing church that we didn't hear the door shut when God left the room. Malachi 1:10 says, "'Oh, that one of you would shut the temple doors, so that you would not light useless fires on my altar! I am not pleased with you,' says the LORD Almighty, 'and I will accept no offering from your hands.'"

> "The unqualified are flawed people, overlooked, but who always rely on the supernatural."
>
> —Adam Kling, youth pastor, Prescott, AZ

Protect the Anointing

It might surprise you to hear it, but I don't believe Samson was a large, muscular man. The Bible doesn't ever say he was. In fact, Delilah had to trick him to find out where he got his strength!

> Some time later, he fell in love with a woman in the Valley of Sorek whose name was Delilah. The rulers of the Philistines went to her and said, "See if you can lure him into showing you the secret of his great strength and how we can overpower him so we may tie him up and subdue him. Each one of us will give you eleven hundred shekels of silver."
>
> —JUDGES 16:4–5

In truth, Samson's covenant was his strength. Without the covenant that kept his anointing firmly in place, he was just an ordinary guy with a lust problem.

We can learn from this that our anointing doesn't remove our flaws; it just sustains us long enough to excuse our humanity. The scariest thing that could ever happen to you, then, is when your gifting continues to flow on stage but your private life becomes full of hypocrisy. Don't believe your press release in the local newspaper of the *Christian Celebrity Times*. Just as soon as you are on the front page, declaring your own works and deeds, you are in danger. You will go from the front page to the obituaries of buried dreams.

When it becomes about the mirror and not looking out the window at a hurting world, we have lost our focus. If it stops being about the lost, then we are in need of being found. We are called to clean up this world, not add to the pollution.

> "Never allow people's negative opinions of you make you feel disqualified when the voice of God has already qualified you. Always make sure God's voice is the loudest voice you listen to."
>
> —Joe Joe Dawson, evangelist, Texarkana, AR

Samson was the anointed judge of Israel, yet he was more concerned about his own desires than God's people, who were in need. We must protect the anointing on our lives! The anointing is worth everything you have to give up in order to keep it! The prophet Isaiah said, "In that day their burden will be lifted from your shoulders, their yoke from your neck; the yoke will be broken because you have grown so fat" (Isa. 10:27). The word translated fat in that verse is *shemen* in the Hebrew,[3] and it can also mean anointing oil.

Jesus spoke of His anointing in Luke 4:18: "The Spirit of the Lord [is] upon Me, because He has anointed Me [the Anointed One, the Messiah] to preach the good news (the Gospel) to the poor; He has sent Me to announce release to the captives and recovery of sight to the blind, to send forth as delivered those who are oppressed [who are down-trodden, bruised, crushed, and broken down by calamity]" (AMP). We know that Jesus is the Christ. The word *Christ* means "Anointed One." It comes from the Greek word *Chrio*, which means "to anoint, consecrating Jesus to the

Messianic office, and furnishing him with the necessary powers for its administration, enduing Christians with the gifts of the Holy Spirit."[4]

The anointing that is on Jesus can be upon every true believer. Jesus gave us His anointing and we share in His suffering, which means we join ourselves to Him. We must protect the anointing from the world that wants to water it down and use it to sunbathe. The oil is not for sunbathing but for empowerment. First John 2:25–27 says, "This is exactly what Christ promised: eternal life, real life! I've written to warn you about those who are trying to deceive you. But they're no match for what is embedded deeply within you—Christ's anointing, no less! You don't need any of their so-called teaching. Christ's anointing teaches you the truth on everything you need to know about yourself and him, uncontaminated by a single lie. Live deeply in what you were taught" (THE MESSAGE).

The anointing that is on your life must be protected. Treasure the anointing!

I love the anointing because it is what allows us to see miracles and testify.

I love the anointing because it is what emboldens every believer to stand for truth, authority, and freedom.

I love the anointing because it is part of God's separation for His chosen.

I love the anointing because it is what empowers the ordinary to walk out a destiny that accomplishes mighty deeds.

I love the anointing because it takes humans made of dirt, embodies them, and allows them to release the unadulterated Word of God.

Samson was anointed to lead a nation, but he refused to protect his anointing. One day he met his undoing, not by a massive army surrounding him, but by a woman who made him feel safe in a place where he should have been on guard.

Three different times Samson teased with Delilah and her

request to know the source of his strength, making up ways for her to tie him up. He fell asleep and she screamed that the Philistines were in the house, and each time he would wake up and break free from the bondages she had placed upon him. Each time she would act offended and nag him even more.

Finally, Samson gave in. The passages says, "Every day she nagged him with her words and pleaded with him until he was tired to death" (Judg. 16:16, MEV). Delilah's name means "one who weakened." She wore Samson out to the point that he quit fighting. Then it was all over! His leadership stopped, and his strength left him. Samson was now just an ordinary guy with great stories of former victories.

Samson's undoing came when his tiredness won. Exhaustion has the ability to make you forget what you are called to be for God. When we refuse to rest, we will become victims of our weariness. When you are tired, you will make decisions you would have never made when you were wide-eyed and awake. That is why we are called to rest in God (Heb. 4:1). When we're tired, we have a tendency to lie down in the wrong places.

> "The unqualified are not propped up by popularity but instead by prayer, don't carry credentials but rather a cross. The unqualified don't demand to make dollars but dream to make a difference. Being unqualified is the very reason that Christ can be glorified through you."
>
> —Scott Jakeway, lay pastor, Phoenix, AZ

Notice When God Leaves

She said, "The Philistines are upon you, Samson." Then he awakened from his sleep and thought, "I will go out as before and shake myself free of them." *He did not know that the Lord had left him.*

—JUDGES 16:20, MEV, EMPHASIS ADDED

Here we read one of the saddest scriptures in the Bible. Samson didn't realize God was gone! But when you play with the enemy, it forces God to walk away. In other words, there comes a point when God will turn you over to yourself (Rom. 1:24). This is the most dangerous place a person could ever end up. God will not be mocked.

Samson was now disqualified. He lost everything that day!

> The Philistines seized him and gouged out his eyes. They took him down to Gaza, bound him with bronze chains, and he ground grain in prison.
>
> —JUDGES 16:21, MEV

Again, the enemy is after our anointing. He is robbing the church of its anointing to use the church for his own gain. He's jealous of what he lost, so his goal is to torture the saints and reduce the called. We must remember this simple equation:

stolen anointing = a powerless church

And it is sad to say, but he is winning. Until crowds, numbers, insecurity, circumstance, and pain cannot rob your anointing from you, you will always sell it off as cheap lip balm to the first voice of compromise. John 10:10 tells us, "The thief comes only to steal and kill and destroy; I have come that they may have life, and have it to the full." Your testimony must be guarded and protected at all times. It is the most valuable tool in your arsenal against Satan: "They overcame him by the blood of the Lamb and by the word of their testimony, and they loved not their lives unto the death" (Rev. 12:11, MEV).

I honestly believe the most embarrassing church service will take place on Judgment Day at the Judgment Seat of

Christ. In that day we will see the works of the flesh burn up in front of the crowd (1 Cor. 3:11–15). Just as Samson was, we'll be rendered powerless and humiliated.

We must wake up from our stupor. God doesn't care how many followers we have on social media or whether or not people like our posts. He wants to know if we followed Him. Did we carry our cross in public or just wear a cross as part of our costume?

> "I would rather be considered unqualified, because when the unqualified are given the chance, they stop at nothing to finish what they have started."
>
> —Austin Marsh, 20, Pell City, AL

The problem is that we often put gifting above integrity. As long as a person has an audience and some Christian jargon, they can make money along with making a mockery of the cross. I often watch Christian performers or celebrity preachers and wonder when the last time was that they had a true encounter with God.

The apostle Paul warned us, though, of what's ahead:

> Don't be naive. There are difficult times ahead. As the end approaches, people are going to be self-absorbed, money-hungry, self-promoting, stuck-up, profane, contemptuous of parents, crude, coarse, dog-eat-dog, unbending, slanderers, impulsively wild, savage, cynical, treacherous, ruthless, bloated windbags, addicted to lust, and allergic to God. They'll make a show of religion, but behind the scenes they're animals. Stay clear of these people.
>
> —2 Timothy 3:1–5, The Message

I must remind you to stay the course. Guard against the anointing invaders, such as lust, fear, lethargy, offense, anger, and greed. The call of God was never designed to give you a license to arrest the sinner while you live in a jail cell called "lost priorities."

You might say, "Now, Pat, we are not supposed to judge." Really? That is not what the Bible says. The Bible says you will be known by your fruit (Matt. 7:16). The apostle Paul said, "What business is it of mine to judge those outside the church? Are you not to judge those inside?" (1 Cor. 5:12). In other words, we are supposed to judge the inside of the church. We must have discernment! Young believers suffer the most when we refuse to call people's lives into accountability. They end up either molested by the lies of the enemy or turned off to faith altogether.

> "Throughout the Bible God used people who were failures, criminals, afraid, poor, dishonest, and cultural outcasts. Our shortcomings don't disqualify us but instead make us prime candidates for receiving the grace required to spread a message of hope to a hurting and broken world. They are those who believed their weaknesses and lack of ability hindered them from having a purpose-filled life but now understand God empowers imperfect people to carry out a perfect plan."
>
> —Matt Armon, media/young adults pastor, Deltona, FL

The Seven Braids

We've established, then, that Samson's strength rested in his hair. In fact, the Bible says that Samson had seven braids of hair in Judges 16:13. I believe those seven braids represent his prayer life, thought life, family life, study life, financial life, ministry life, and physical life. These are the seven most crucial areas of our lives. The enemy would love to cut off your braids. You must take the scissors out of the hands of the enemy and declare, "You can't cut my hair!" No more bald churches! Why? Psalm 133:2 says that the oil flows down the head to the beard to the body. The hair is your filter!

Fortunately, at Samson's very worst moment, at the place where he would be taken captive for twenty years, something miraculous happened. His hair began to grow!

> But the hair on his head began to grow again after it had been shaved.
> —JUDGES 16:22

That tells us no matter how we may have messed up and failed, God will restore us. He'll return what's been robbed. And it's true. That's what happened with Samson.

Let's take a look at what happened. One day the Philistines decided they wanted to make a show of God's fallen warrior:

> Now the rulers of the Philistines assembled to offer a great sacrifice to Dagon their god and to celebrate, saying, "Our god has delivered Samson, our enemy, into our hands." When the people saw him, they praised their god, saying, "Our god has delivered our enemy into our hands, the one who laid waste our land and multiplied our slain." While they were in high spirits, they shouted, "Bring out Samson to entertain us." So they called Samson out of the prison, and he performed for them.
> —JUDGES 16:23–25

Can you see the spectacle? People were wildly drunk. Samson was no longer a part of the crowd he used to party with. They were taunting, "Look at this guy who used to torture us. Ha ha!" The crowd erupted as they saw Samson. There he was, blind and broken down, but what they didn't realize was that God is a God of covenant.

Suddenly Samson said to a young boy, "Would you place

my hands on the two pillars?" These pillars supported the entire roof of the stadium. Then Samson prayed:

> "Lord God, remember me, I pray! Please strengthen me just this once, God, so that I may get full revenge on the Philistines for my two eyes!" Then Samson grasped the two middle pillars on which the temple was set and leaned against them, one with his right hand and one with his left. Samson said, "Let me die with the Philistines!" He pushed with all his strength, and the temple fell upon the rulers and all the people who were in it. At his death he killed more than he had killed in his life.
>
> —Judges 16:28–30, mev

God restored His covenant with Samson. He gave him victory at the end.

This account in God's Word shows us that regardless of how far down you fall, our God will pick you up. You may have been disqualified, but that means you've become part of the unqualified who can now rise up and lead. That's what we've been here to prove all along.

Cry out, "Devil, you can't cut my hair!" The hair of the Samson church is growing again!

Chapter 11

THE LION, THE CORPSE, AND THE DONKEY

"Acknowledging that you are unqualified is not the same as admitting failure. It's relieving the pressure to be something that you're not. To be unqualified is simply to acknowledge that in order to succeed, a greater power than you must step in. Those who refuse to acknowledge that they are unqualified are the ones who will inevitably fail."

—Nate Schatzline, youth pastor, The House, Modesto, CA

THERE IS A story in the Bible that I dare say I've never heard anyone preach about. The story barely makes a blip on the screen of great Bible stories. It's as ancient as the Old Testament prophets but as relevant as the mega-churches that now list their weekly attendance in magazines that are supposed to be about outreach. It's a story of a no-name young prophet who, in one day, changed the course of an entire kingdom—and then ended up losing it all. This story is a story of alarm. It will remind us that the calling of God is wonderful to behold but is also so easily abandoned!

The story starts out so promising. Like a bolt of light-ning, this prophet shows up in town to confront an idol-worshipping king. The king's name was Jeroboam. Just as the king was about to make a sacrifice on the altar, the unnamed prophet walks in and interrupts.

> A man of God came out of Judah to Bethel by the word of the Lord while Jeroboam stood by the altar to burn incense. He cried against the altar by the word of the Lord and said, "O altar, altar, thus says the Lord: 'A child named Josiah will be born in the house of David, and he will sacrifice upon you the priests of the high places who burn incense on you, and these men's bones shall be burned upon you.'" He gave a sign the same day, saying, "This is the sign that the Lord has spoken: 'The altar will be torn apart, and the ashes that are upon it will be poured out.'"
>
> —1 Kings 13:1–3, mev

Can you imagine? Here is an unqualified and unknown prophet suddenly confronting an evil king!

The Bible says the king immediately started to attack the prophet. This is proof that the message you give from the Lord will surely cause you to gain enemies.

> When King Jeroboam heard the saying of the man of God who had cried against the altar in Bethel, he reached out his hand from the altar, saying, "Arrest him!" And the hand that he put forth against him dried up so that he could not pull it back in again. The altar also was torn, and the ashes poured out from the altar, just as the man of God had said it would as a sign of the Lord.
>
> —1 Kings 13:4–5, mev

Wow! This is powerful! The prophet gives the message, the king's hand withers up, and the altar is split in two. This would be enough to make any young minister snap pictures, hold a press conference, or at least send out a newsletter.

Then the king did something remarkable. He asked the young prophet to pray for his hand to be healed—and do you know what? He did, and the king's hand was healed. How many times in ministry have you been asked to help those who tried to harm you? Could you do it? This prophet did.

The sticking point of this story—the part that disrupts my spirit so much—is that this should have been the prophet's greatest day ever. But as we will see, it didn't end well. This no-name prophet's greatest day of ministry ended up being his last!

Might we, as the unqualified, learn something from his demise?

The Path to a Forgotten Ministry

Let's take a look at seven points to glean from this story of the prophet from Judah who went from the height of heights to his downfall on the same day. Some of his choices were good; some of them were less good. They all have something to teach us.

1. You can't allow your anointing to be bought.

In 1 Kings 13 the king tries to get the prophet to eat with him, which God had forbidden. We read in verses 7–10: "'Come home with me for a meal, and I will give you a gift.' But the man of God answered the king, 'Even if you were to give me half your possessions, I would not go with you, nor would I eat bread or drink water here. For I was commanded by the word of the LORD: "You must not eat bread or drink water or return by the way you came."' So he took another road and did not return by the way he had come to Bethel."

When God gives us mandates, we must always watch for the traps of the enemy. As soon as the prophet restored the king's hand, the prophet's mandate from God was challenged. The king wanted to buy his influence. This shows us that just because we walk in a supernatural anointing, we are never immune from the enemy's attack. In fact, it is after we have been used by God that we must stand the strongest.

God had given the unknown prophet guidelines to protect

him from outside influences and to keep his message pure. So the prophet immediately stood his ground when the king made his offer. He refused to be bought. He understood that without God's help his mission would be compromised. As a traveling minister who often stays in hotels, I have learned that I must always stay on guard.

There have been times when I knew the enemy was trying to take me out. All he needs is a little compromise for a minster to become another fallen voice. Once when I was getting off an elevator, I was propositioned by a woman. Not only did I ignore this woman, but when the elevator stopped at my floor I ran as fast as I could to my room. That experience taught me to never again get on an elevator alone with the opposite sex. Integrity calls us to guard our lives when compromise knocks the loudest.

2. As the anointing on you grows, the interruptions get louder.

Watch what happens when the prophet heads out of town. First Kings 13:11–15 says, "Now there lived an old prophet in Bethel, and his sons came and told him all that the man of God had done that day in Bethel. They also told their father the words that he had spoken to the king. Their father said to them, 'What way did he go?' For his sons had seen the way the man of God who came from Judah had gone. He said to his sons, 'Saddle my donkey.' So they saddled the donkey for him, and he rode on it. He went after the man of God and found him sitting under an oak, and he said to him, 'Are you the man of God who came from Judah?' And he said, 'I am.' Then he said to him, 'Come home with me and eat bread'" (MEV).

Oftentimes it is the simplest distraction that begins to break down your will. The Bible says that an old prophet came and found the prophet. The most dangerous people to the body of Christ are those who have tasted the anointing and have for some reason walked away. This old prophet wanted to have influence in the prophet's life. I believe that he was sent from the enemy to quiet the messenger. The prophet once again recited his mandate, but religion would blind him from the truth.

3. You must stay true to your mandate from God.

In 1 Kings 13:17–20 the prophet from Judah says, "I have been told by the word of the LORD: 'You must not eat bread or drink water there or return by the way you came.' The old prophet answered, 'I too am a prophet, as you are. And an angel said to me by the word of the LORD: "Bring him back with you to your house so that he may eat bread and drink water."' (But he was lying to him.) So the man of God returned with him and ate and drank in his house. While they were sitting at the table, the word of the LORD came to the old prophet who had brought him back."

We must learn to walk in supernatural discernment at all times. The old prophet was a liar with an agenda. I cannot tell you how many times I have heard the Lord say to me just about the time I was joining in relationship with someone, "Pat, stay away from that person. He has an agenda that is not Holy Spirit led." This has kept me from many trials. Other times I have ignored the voice of God, and it caused me pain. Just because someone says he is from God does not mean he is from God. Don't ignore that little alarm that goes off when you are joining in relationship with the wrong person.

This old prophet was seeking to own an anointing he had lost. The prophet made the fatal mistake of ignoring his mandate from God. It would cost him his life. This is one of the reasons the Bible tells us to pray in the Spirit on all occasions (Eph. 6:18). It is when we engage our spirit with God's Spirit that we are able to walk in discernment.

4. When you compromise, the whole room will know it.

At this point in the story, the meal is suddenly interrupted with a prophetic word from the backslidden old prophet. We read in 1 Kings 13:21–22, "He cried out to the man of

God who had come from Judah, 'This is what the LORD says: "You have defied the word of the LORD and have not kept the command the LORD your God gave you. You came back and ate bread and drank water in the place where he told you not to eat or drink. Therefore your body will not be buried in the tomb of your ancestors."''

We know that the Bible says in Romans 11:29 that the gifts and calling of God are irrevocable. This old prophet still walked in an anointing from above. The old prophet began to declare that the unknown prophet would pay a price for his disobedience. I have often said that compromise is the loudest voice in the room! Why? Because it eventually tells on itself. Everyone in the room heard the prophetic decree of judgment. It was over for the prophet sent from God. This is why we must make up our minds to stand firm, because if we don't we will face the embarrassment that comes with compromise.

5. Your gifts and ministry can betray you.

The story goes on in 1 Kings 13:23–30:

> When the man of God had finished eating and drinking, the prophet who had brought him back saddled his donkey for him. As he went on his way, a lion met him on the road and killed him, and his body was left lying on the road, with both the donkey and the lion standing beside it. Some people who passed by saw the body lying there, with the lion standing beside the body, and they went and reported it in the city where the old prophet lived.
>
> When the prophet who had brought him back from his journey heard of it, he said, "It is the man of God who defied the word of the LORD. The LORD has given him over to the lion, which has mauled him and killed him, as the word of the LORD had warned him."
>
> The prophet said to his sons, "Saddle the donkey for me," and they did so. Then he went out and found the

> body lying on the road, with the donkey and the lion
> standing beside it. The lion had neither eaten the body
> nor mauled the donkey. So the prophet picked up the
> body of the man of God, laid it on the donkey, and
> brought it back to his own city to mourn for him and
> bury him. Then he laid the body in his own tomb, and
> they mourned over him and said, "Alas, my brother!"

We must realize that even though we are anointed and full of the power of God, we can still end up a corpse on the side of the road. Our faith must not be in our gifts or calling, but always in Jesus. The prophet ended up dead on his greatest day of ministry. He ignored God's mandates and bought into a lie from the enemy. I have seen this happen to so many who were full of amazing God potential. They have ended up as a memorial on the highway of holiness because somewhere along the way compromise took hold.

6. The tomb of yesterday's ministry is full of lost potential.

First Kings 13:31–32 says, "After burying him, he [the old prophet] said to his sons, 'When I die, bury me in the grave where the man of God is buried; lay my bones beside his bones. For the message he declared by the word of the LORD against the altar in Bethel and against all the shrines on the high places in the towns of Samaria will certainly come true.'"

Lying in the tomb was a man who should have been used by God for years. Instead, his body became another epitaph written by the enemy on a life that wasn't done. He started out so great and ended up a dead prophet full of potential. When we die we should do so with nothing left to do. We should have fulfilled all that God had for us. When we get to heaven, we should be empty. God orders our steps, but Satan does everything he can to shorten them. That's why we must stay focused on the mission God has given us.

7. Don't be known for your last sermon.

Interestingly 1 Kings 13:33–34 tells us, "Even after this, Jeroboam did not change his evil ways, but once more appointed priests for the high places from all sorts of people. Anyone who wanted to become a priest he consecrated for the high places. This was the sin of the house of Jeroboam that led to its downfall and to its destruction from the face of the earth." We know that the prophet died prematurely and his influence died with him. Soon after his demise, the king forgot the message he brought. This is a powerful lesson that shows us that if the enemy can take us out, he can take out our message. This is why God has called us to finish strong.

Stay the Course!

Now, let's recap this story. The unknown prophet confronts the king, and the king is healed after he tries to attack the messenger. The king then tries to get the prophet to stay, but the prophet lets him know that he has strict orders from God that he must not eat with anyone and that he must not return home the same way he had come. On his way home he is approached by a backslidden old prophet while he is relaxing under a tree. The old prophet lies to him and convinces him to come home with him. When they get to the old prophet's house they begin to eat supper. The old prophet interrupts the meal with a word from God. The word was that the unknown prophet would not go down in history as one of the great prophets.

The unknown prophet then gets up to go home. On his way home a lion attacks him and kills him. The old prophet gets word that the unknown prophet is dead, and he gets on a donkey to see the scene of the attack. When he arrives he sees a lion, a corpse, and a donkey. This in itself went against the laws of nature. Wasn't the lion hungry? Why didn't he eat the donkey? Could it be the lion was simply satisfied with destroying the messenger? First Peter 5:8 warns,

"Be alert and of sober mind. Your enemy the devil prowls around like a roaring lion looking for someone to devour."

The reason I called this chapter "The Lion, the Corpse, and the Donkey" is because that is what was found at the scene of the accident.

The lion represents the prophet's anointing. He was bold and courageous.

The corpse symbolized a vessel that once had power in it.

The donkey was the prophet's vehicle and represented his ministry.

I must admit, this story has bothered me greatly since I first learned of it. It wasn't supposed to end the way it did. This unknown prophet should have been great! He should have gone down in the history books, like Samuel, Isaiah, and Amos. There should be a book of the Bible named after him. Yet in one day he was destroyed—literally—because he listened to the wrong voice.

The truth is, what happened to him could happen to any one of us. We, the unqualified, could meet an unexpected end that lacks redemption. I've seen it happen before, and maybe you have too.

I wonder how many people could have been great, but somewhere along the way they got tripped up. Galatians 5:7 says, "You were running a good race. Who cut in on you to keep you from obeying the truth?" The enemy wants you to have moments of sorrow that should have been testimonies of overcoming! Proverbs 28:19 tells us, "But those who chase fantasies will have their fill of poverty." You must stand firm!

God has called you to be on guard. You're not in this fight alone! First Peter 5:9–11 tells us, "Keep your guard up. You're not the only ones plunged into these hard times. It's the same with Christians all over the world. So keep a firm grip on the faith. The suffering won't last forever. It won't be long before this generous God who has great plans for us in Christ—eternal and glorious plans they are!—will have you put together and on your feet for good. He gets the last word; yes, he does" (THE MESSAGE).

The unknown prophet would end up being buried with the old prophet who had lied to him. He missed out on his own place of rest. We must always keep in mind that there is a prize that awaits those of us who finish the race. Heaven is watching us. The great cloud of witnesses is hanging over the balcony of heaven chanting, "We finished our race! Will you?"

I will never forget something the Lord spoke to me once when I was at the gym working out. I had worship playing in my headphones and suddenly the Lord said, "Pat, never desire to hear the cheer of the crowd but listen for the cries of the cloud, the great cloud of witnesses. These are those who cheer on the saints and pour out the bowls of prayers."

We must stay the course and ignore the distractions. When we ignore the voice of the Lord we are setting ourselves up for devastation. We are the unqualified who must not get disqualified!

I challenge you to listen to the voice of God first. Stay on course. Don't become a wreck on the side of the road for everyone to look at. There is one more thing in this story that haunts me. It is something said in 1 Kings 13:30. After the old prophet loaded the body of the unknown prophet on his donkey and returned to his town, he placed the prophet's body in his own tomb. Then the verse says, "The people mourned, saying, 'A sad day, brother!'" (THE MESSAGE). A sad day, indeed. We must not let this be said of us. We must finish what we started for God!

SECTION IV

THE RISE OF THE UNQUALIFIED

Chapter 12

GET YOUR FEET READY

> "The unqualified are those who move forward with the little they have instead of waiting on the much they will never receive. The unqualified fight through the turbulence of 'Get more qualifications' and live powerfully in the God-pleasing reality of 'My little is enough.'"
>
> —Britt Hancock, missionary, founder of Mountain Gateway

THERE'S NOTHING MORE exciting than seeing someone rise up out of nowhere and suddenly be a powerful voice of awakening for God. Nevertheless, as previously stated, we know there is no such thing as a true "suddenly." The truth is, God was developing that leader over long seasons and dark nights to be His voice.

The touch of God is so evident when leaders like this minister God's Word that a holy fear of the Lord often enters the room. The saints used to call it a holy hush. With fire in their spirits and brokenness as their nameplate, they stir the dying embers of past revivals and ignite the wood of broken crosses. We must have these types of leaders rise up once again—those who refuse to compromise for tainted applause. We need leaders whose lives scream holiness without their saying a word. Proverbs 11:30 says, "The fruit of the [uncompromisingly] righteous is a tree of life, and he who is wise captures human lives [for God, as a fisher of men—he gathers and receives them for eternity]" (AMP).

These leaders are the ones usually jeered as unqualified by the self-righteous and relegated to small stages by the pious. But they are embraced by the desperate. I believe God takes joy in placing favor upon them as He removes favor from those who no longer bow to Him but save their curtsy for court jesters.

They are the true unqualified.

And you could be one of them.

As I hope has been made plain by now, we need more of these leaders to rise up now—the true unqualified who refuse to compromise for the acceptance of a tainted applause but instead rely on the power of God to course through their lives and change the world.

So, how do you get there?

Well, let me ask you this. Have you ever felt like you were sitting on the edge of a breakthrough? Like something was about to happen but just hadn't burst through to the surface yet? I've spent my entire life feeling this way. Truthfully, I've learned it's how the Holy Spirit keeps us stirred up for our next level of growth. If we let ourselves stay there, waiting for the next move of God, we'll be ready to move when others have grown all too comfortable with the status quo.

While we're waiting for that breakthrough, even when the heavens seem silent, it's important that we not give up. This is the time to keep pressing in and chasing the heart of God. Great revivals in history usually took place just about the moment the leader was ready to call it quits. It's as if God waits until nothing is left but empty vessels waiting to be filled. I often wonder how many people have given up or stopped only one step away from their breakthrough. That's usually when the "bam!" moment hits.

> Friends, when life gets really difficult, don't jump to the conclusion that God isn't on the job. Instead, be

glad that you are in the very thick of what Christ experienced. This is a spiritual refining process, with glory just around the corner.

—1 Peter 4:12–13, The Message

> "Because of the great love of our God, the unqualified are propelled into becoming the qualified. Harvest time is here, and the qualified are standing strong and ready for this last harvest. If I know anything at all, it is that God's love for us changes and covers every part of our life and purpose here on earth. We must understand that God has put greatness in all of us. We must discover how to use it for His glory!"
>
> —Margaret Edmondson, minister and entrepreneur, Albertville, AL

The Message of the Nail

I found myself on the cusp of one of those breakthrough moments on July 4, 2012. I was ministering in El Paso, Texas, that day, but all I could think about was what day it was. I left my hotel to go for a jog, and as I jogged, I began to complain to the Lord. I said, "God, it isn't fair. I should be at home with my family doing what millions of Americans are doing today. I should be sitting around the barbeque grill cooking up a feast and having fun. Why am I in El Paso?"

God didn't answer.

Then I looked down and saw an old, bent, rusted nail in the road. I stopped to pick it up because I didn't want anyone to get a flat tire.

That's when God chose to speak. He said, "That nail represents the nail that I took in My feet for you. I was nailed to a tree so that you could run."

As I jogged, I continued to hold the nail and began to

notice I was rejoicing to carry it. It was a physical reminder of the message of hope I was there in El Paso—and everywhere else God leads me to minister—to carry to the hurting.

Christ was nailed to a tree so we could run. Just think about that. The day of hoping someday God will use you is over. God already wants to use you and has prepared the way to do so through the Son's death on the cross. His pierced feet give you feet that can run the race!

A Piercing God Prepared For

As I jogged that day, I kept growing more and more overwhelmed with this idea. Jesus allowed His feet to be nailed down so I could run. But really God had promised this would happen all along—all the way back in the Garden of Eden, when God confronted the snake that had deceived Adam and Eve. God said to Satan, "And I will put enmity between you and the woman, and between your offspring and hers; he will crush your head, and you will strike his heel" (Gen. 3:15).

This was the shot heard around eternity. Satan was warned of his own demise. Yet this did not deter him. It should have, but it didn't. Because even the very genealogy of man tells how this story ends.

I know, I know. We don't usually enjoy reading the "begats" of the Bible. It can get really boring. But it turns out when you look a little closer, it's actually pretty amazing! God's redemption story is spelled out right there on the page— right there in the mix of all that begetting.

Take a look at each name and what each one means: Adam (man), begat Seth (appointed), begat Enosh (mortal), begat Kenan (sorrow), begat Mahalalel (blessed God), begat Jared (shall come down), begat Enoch (teaching), begat Methuselah (his death shall bring), begat Lamech (the despairing), begat Noah (rest and comfort).[1]

What does this mean? String the meanings together, and you get this: "Man [is] appointed mortal sorrow, [but] the blessed God shall come down, teaching that His death shall bring the despairing rest and comfort."

Wow! God truly did have a plan! In the midst of utter chaos and destruction amongst God's creation, there was still a plan of redemption. There was always a plan for Jesus to become our redemption—to be pierced so we can run.

We must keep running. Trust that God will take care of the enemy. Very soon, in fact, the devil will feel the feet he pierced stand upon his head.

> I couldn't be more proud of you!—I want you also to be smart, making sure every "good" thing is the real thing. Don't be gullible in regard to smooth-talking evil. Stay alert like this, and before you know it the God of peace will come down on Satan with both feet, stomping him into the dirt. Enjoy the best of Jesus!
> —ROMANS 16:19–20, THE MESSAGE

When You Stumble, Get Back Up!

It probably won't surprise you to hear that the Bible talks a great deal about running the race. I believe God is so invested in us that He continually speaks on this subject. And the most important thing for the unqualified to remember is to never stop short of your calling. (Remember that lesson from the no-name prophet in the last chapter?)

Paul puts it this way:

> But you, Timothy, man of God: Run for your life from all this. Pursue a righteous life—a life of wonder, faith, love, steadiness, courtesy. Run hard and fast in the faith. Seize the eternal life, the life you were called to, the life you so fervently embraced in the presence of so many witnesses."
> —1 TIMOTHY 6:11–12, THE MESSAGE

The enemy knows we're all aiming to stay the course, though, so he's doing his very best to trip us up each step of the way. But God has a plan to keep us from the traps. Proverbs 3:26 says, "For the Lord shall be your confidence, firm and strong, and shall keep your foot from being caught [in a trap or some hidden danger]" (AMP).

Sin has a way of causing massive wrecks on the paths we're called to run. And our stumbling can cause others to stumble too. We've got to hang on so others don't trip either!

> So don't sit around on your hands! No more dragging your feet! Clear the path for long-distance runners so no one will trip and fall, so no one will step in a hole and sprain an ankle. Help each other out. And run for it!
> —HEBREWS 12:12–13, THE MESSAGE

We're called to carry our cross and follow in the steps of Jesus (1 Pet. 2:21). God wants you to chase Him! And if you keep your eyes on God, you won't trip over your feet (Ps. 25:15).

If, by chance, you're reading this book and have fallen down, then stand up and run back toward God. He's waiting on you. No more excuses! No more dancing with the world. God will renew your strength.

> Let God work his will in you. Yell a loud no to the Devil and watch him scamper. Say a quiet yes to God and he'll be there in no time. Quit dabbling in sin. Purify your inner life. Quit playing the field. Hit bottom, and cry your eyes out. The fun and games are over. Get serious, really serious. Get down on your knees before the Master; it's the only way you'll get on your feet.
> —JAMES 4:7–10, THE MESSAGE

What Story Will Your Feet Tell?

Our feet should tell the story of our journey when we are laid to rest. I hope my feet say, "He stayed the course!"

My feet have stood on the shores of Asia, the mountains

of South America, the barrios of Central America, the ice of Alaska, the golden sand of Australia, and the asphalt roads of America but, most importantly, they have knelt in the presence of my King at His feet. This is my daily cry:

> I'm asking GOD for one thing, only one thing: To live with him in his house my whole life long. I'll contemplate his beauty; I'll study at his feet.
> —PSALM 27:4, THE MESSAGE

We must get our feet ready! Ephesians 6:15 says, "And having shod your feet in preparation [to face the enemy with the firm-footed stability, the promptness, and the readiness produced by the good news] of the Gospel of peace" (AMP).

This is the greatest hour in which we could ever be alive. I have never seen such a hunger for God as I see now in this generation. Our church services are often interrupted with hundreds or even thousands running to the altar. I never get used to it. The desperation I have personally seen is at an all-time high as people desire to have an encounter with their Creator. Will you be able to declare with Paul, "I have fought the good fight, I have finished the race, I have kept the faith" (2 Tim. 4:7)?

We, the unqualified, are His feet! The blood and the nail make a way for us to carry His message. Where will your feet carry you?

Chapter 13

YOU ARE GOD'S HASHTAG

#wearetheunqualified

O NE OF MY favorite things to do is read the hashtags at the end of a tweet or Instagram post. Have you ever noticed people using the number sign, or pound sign, along with a statement (squished together as one long word) at the end of their tweets or Instagram photo captions? This is what is known as a *hashtag*.

When I first discovered hashtags, I thought they were so silly—until I understood what they were for. The hashtag first became a phenomenon on Twitter around 2009 and then began circulating on the other social media websites. They make it possible to group messages on a similar topic together, as clicking on the hashtag returns a set of messages that contain all the posts on that platform using that particular hashtag. It's a way for people search out other posts on the same topic. We did this a great deal with my last book, *I Am Remnant*, by posting #iamremnant with pictures or quotes on social media. This allowed others to follow the hashtag and know what was happening with the remnant vision.

Hashtags also provide a way to get a further message or idea across. For instance, people may post a picture or state-ment in their status update and then add a hashtag with another word, statement, or opinion that helps deepen our understanding of their original post even more. For instance, someone may post a tweet that says, "The football game was incredible!" and then add #wearethechampions at the end of it. That way others know the game was incredible because it led to that person's team winning a championship. Or someone may post a picture of their spouse on Instagram and hashtag the picture with #mytruelove. The hashtag expresses a deeper sentiment or opinion than the picture does on its own.

> "The unqualified is so obscure, so unprepared from man's perspective, that he/she isn't even on the devil's radar! They have no pedigree, no endorsements, no reputation. They are free from the expectations or judgments of critics."
>
> —Glenn Randall, lead pastor, Albertville, AL

You're a Living Hashtag

My point here is that you are God's hashtag. Every time God gets ready to use you, He begins by changing your story and adding what's missing. He has the ability to change the outcome of what the enemy meant for evil to reflect His divine intervention. And when God gets involved, it becomes His story!

Behind every unqualified person is the qualifying factor that God intervened. History is your testimony of where you have been. If your history is like mine, then you know you're a walking miracle.

Your life has hashtags all over it! The moment-in-time pictures and statements about your life do not tell the whole story until God adds the hashtag. Just read the promises of God and you'll realize there are hashtags beside every one. For instance, check out this passage in Romans 5:

> There's more to come: We continue to shout our praise even when we're hemmed in with troubles, because we know how troubles can develop passionate patience in us, and how that patience in turn forges the tempered

steel of virtue, keeping us alert for whatever God will do next. In alert expectancy such as this, we're never left feeling shortchanged. Quite the contrary—we can't round up enough containers to hold everything God generously pours into our lives through the Holy Spirit!
—Romans 5:3–5, The Message
#itaintover

"It is the unqualified that can trace our dreams come true back to childhood moments when God dropped seeds of passion into our unassuming lives. Ours were fragile, tender shoots that no one even expected to survive. Yet deep in our humanity, 'God-ness' was engrafted and cultivated by the Holy Spirit. Anyone who knew us back then are awed when lives are affected by us today—we, most of all. The staggering wonder of seeing God working in us and through us is the humbling mystery of the unqualified."

—Tava Brice, pastor, Fayetteville, NC

I've been blessed to stand on hundreds of stages ministering the gospel but, really, that is only part of the story. If you see someone on stage, you most likely don't know where they came from and what they've walked through. The lights on the stage that shine upon their armor tend to pixelate the real image. The truth of their struggle to get to the stage is usually avoided or forgotten because success has a short memory. Nevertheless, there are what I call "hashtags" that are closely behind every person who stands up to lead. They are not always visible, but the hashtags are there. These are the statements that really define who you are.

The key is realizing that without God, we would never have a stage or platform in the first place. It is when we begin to believe we can do it without Him that we end up dancing in the ballroom alone. What do I mean? Because I am so unqualified, I must always remind myself that without God, I am just an echo of what I should have become. This forces me to rely on Him at all times.

The apostle Paul said it best:

> This is my life work: helping people understand and respond to this Message. It came as a sheer gift to me, a real surprise, God handling all the details. When it came to presenting the Message to people who had no background in God's way, I was the least qualified of any of the available Christians. God saw to it that I was equipped, but you can be sure that it had nothing to do with my natural abilities.
> —EPHESIANS 3:7–8, THE MESSAGE
> #ididntdoitonmyown

> "It's the unqualified that God breaks in order to show humility and then builds in order to show others what humility looks like."
>
> —Deniecea David, 19, ministry student, Richmond, VA

The best way to stay balanced in your life for God is to realize there's always a hashtag telling the rest of your story. Jesus became our greatest hashtag! When there was no hope for mankind, when the devil thought he had won, Jesus showed up to make a show of him. He added to the story!

> And having disarmed the powers and authorities, he made a public spectacle of them, triumphing over them by the cross.
> —COLOSSIANS 2:15
> #jesusdontplay

Jesus gives us the victory over whatever we may face. Even when the enemy attacks and comes after you, God will give you the ability to praise Him. He is right there with you. This psalm passage proves it, and it assures us:

> God, don't just watch from the sidelines. Come on! Run to my side! My accusers—make them lose face. Those out to get me—make them look like idiots, while I stretch out, reaching for you, and daily add praise to praise. I'll write the book on your righteousness, talk up your salvation the livelong day, never run out of good things to write or say. I come in the power of the Lord GOD, I post signs marking his right-of-way.
> —PSALM 71:12–16, THE MESSAGE
> #addpraisetoyourpraise
> #watchthesigns

You have to realize that whatever you are going through can't define you. The moment you realize you are God's hashtag, the end of the story changes. The enemy never counted on the hashtag! God adds to the story He will help you finish:

> There has never been the slightest doubt in my mind that the God who started this great work in you would keep at it and bring it to a flourishing finish on the very day Christ Jesus appears.
> —PHILIPPIANS 1:6, THE MESSAGE
> #yourenotdoneyet

Do you realize we're living in the last days? If you don't, then all you have to do is turn on the radio, read a newspaper, or watch the news to realize time is running out. Whether it's a disease pandemic, an economic collapse, a terrorist attack, or nature's fury on display, we can see things are not good! I'm convinced more than ever that we are most likely the generation that will not see death. Very soon the eternal history books will be written, and I believe we are in the last chapter. We are the exclamation point God is placing at the end of time.

This should excite every fiber of our bodies. It should awaken us to the fact that God trusts us with His final message. You could have been born at any time in history, but you are alive now. You have to do something with your life, because you are part of God's finishing touch on creation.

> But make sure that you don't get so absorbed and exhausted in taking care of all your day-by-day obligations that you lose track of the time and doze off, oblivious to God. The night is about over, dawn is about to break. Be up and awake to what God is doing! God is putting the finishing touches on the salvation work he began when we first believed. We can't afford to waste a minute, must not squander these precious daylight hours in frivolity and indulgence, in sleeping around and dissipation, in bickering and grabbing everything in sight. Get out of bed and get dressed! Don't loiter and linger, waiting until the very last minute. Dress yourselves in Christ, and be up and about!
> —ROMANS 13:11–14, THE MESSAGE
> #godisstillworkingonyou

You and I are the finishing touches! We are the last part of the equation. We are God's final statement. We are His hashtag!

Not only will God add to your story when you live a life that chases after His heart, but when you decide to walk away from God, there are also hashtags that follow you. For instance, look at these Scripture truths:

> You're not getting by with anything. Every refusal and avoidance of God adds fuel to the fire. The day is coming when it's going to blaze hot and high, God's fiery and righteous judgment. Make no mistake: In the end you get what's coming to you—Real Life for those who work on God's side, but to those who insist

on getting their own way and take the path of least
resistance, Fire!
                            —Romans 2:5–8, The Message
                                            #thefireisreal

The Angel said to me, "Write this: 'Blessed are those
invited to the Wedding Supper of the Lamb.'" He
added, "These are the true words of God!"
                          —Revelation 19:9, The Message
                                    #godsayswhatgodmeans

Lastly, we must never doubt our calling. We do not possess that right!

I will close this book as I have my last two books. This
quote is in my private study, and I read it nearly every week.
It is from a man who led a movement of the unqualified
nearly one hundred fifty years ago!

"Not called!" did you say? "Not heard the call," I think
you should say. Put your ear down to the Bible, and
hear Him bid you go and pull sinners out of the fire of
sin. Put your ear down to the burdened, agonized heart
of humanity, and listen to its pitiful wail for help. Go
stand by the gates of hell, and hear the damned entreat
you to go to their father's house and bid their brothers
and sisters and servants and masters not to come
there. Then look Christ in the face—whose mercy you
have professed to obey—and tell Him whether you will
join heart and soul and body and circumstances in the
march to publish His mercy to the world.[1]
                                    —William Booth
                          Founder, The Salvation Army
                                    #nomoreexcuses

The Prayer of the Unqualified

Dear Jesus,
*   I come before You with not much to offer. I*
simply desire to know You and be led by You. My

entire life has culminated in this moment in time. I ask that You anoint me for such a time as this. I will stand for You at all times. Your Word shall be my very core, and Your precepts shall guide me. It doesn't matter what others think or whether or not I am qualified, because with You on my side, all things are possible. I am Your servant. Keep my heart, mind, body, and spirit free of the pollution of this world. On this day I declare that I am ready to lead a Holy Spirit revolution. Let me see the wave of Your Spirit overtake this nation and world. I am the unqualified remnant of today. Therefore, I am equipped to do the impossible for God. Amen!

NOTES

Introduction

1. Smith Wigglesworth, *Smith Wigglesworth Devotional* comp. and ed. Patricia Culbertson (New Kensington, PA: Whitaker House, 1999), 225.

Chapter 1
"Ah, Sovereign Lord!"

1. Dictionary.com, s.v. "ah," http://dictionary.reference.com/browse/ah! (accessed January 26, 2015).

2. Eliyah.com, "Commentary on Bible Prefaces," http://www.eliyah.com/compref.html (accessed January 26, 2015).

3. Preceptautstin.org, "Adonai-Lord-The Name of God," http://www.preceptaustin.org/adonai-lord-the_name_of_god.htm (accessed January 26, 2015).

4. Preceptautstin.org, "Jehovah-I Am," http://www.preceptaustin.org/jehovah_-_i_am.htm (accessed January 26, 2015).

5. Agape Bible Study, "The Many Names of God," http://www.agapebiblestudy.com/documents/the%20many%20names%20of%20god.htm (accessed January 26, 2015).

6. *Burwell v. Hobby Lobby Stores, Inc.* http://www.scotusblog.com/case-files/cases/sebelius-v-hobby-lobby-stores-inc/ (accessed January 26, 2015).

7. Goodreads.com, "Dietrich Bonhoeffer Quotes," http://www.goodreads.com/author/quotes/29333.Dietrich_Bonhoeffer (accessed January 26, 2015).

8. USdebtclock.org, "US National Debt," http://www.usdebtclock.org/ (accessed January 26, 2015).

9. Whitehouse.gov, "Joint Press Availability With President Obama and President Gul of Turkey," http://www.whitehouse.gov/the_press_office/Joint-Press-Availability-With-President-Obama-And-President-Gul-Of-Turkey/ (accessed January 26, 2015); Kathleen Gilbert and John-Henry Westen, "Obama: We Do Not Consider Ourselves a Christian Nation," Life Site News, https://www.lifesitenews.com/news/obama-we-do-not-consider-ourselves-a-christian-nation (accessed January 26, 2015).

10. Nile Gardiner and Morgan Lorraine Roach, "Barack Obama's Top 10 Apologies: How the President Has Humiliated a Superpower," The Heritage Foundation, http://www.heritage.org/research/reports/2009/06/barack-obamas-top-10-apologies-how-the-president-has-humiliated-a-superpower (accessed January 26, 2015).

11. Glenn Greenwald, "Obama, the US and the Muslim World: The Animosity Deepens," The Guardian, http://www.theguardian.com/commentisfree/2013/feb/15/us-obama-muslims-animosity-deepens (accessed January 26, 2015).

12. Archives.gov, "Declaration of Independence," http://www.archives.gov/exhibits/charters/declaration_transcript.html (accessed January 26, 2015).

13. The Heritage Foundation, "Thanksgiving Proclamation," http://www.heritage.org/initiatives/first-principles/primary-sources/washingtons-thanksgiving-proclamation (accessed January 26, 2015).

14. USA Christian Ministries, "US History Quotes About God and the Bible," http://www.usachristianministries.com/us-history-quotes-about-god-and-the-bible/ (accessed January 26, 2015).

15. Ibid.

16. Ibid.

17. Ibid.

18. Ibid.

19. Abrahamlincolnonline, "The Gettysburg Address," http://www.abrahamlincolnonline.org/lincoln/speeches/gettysburg.htm (accessed January 26, 2015).

20. As quoted in Kenneth D. Wald, Allison Calhoun-Brown, *Religion and Politics in the United States* (Lanham, MD: Rowman & Littlefield, 2014), 58.

21. Ronald Reagan Presidential Library and Museum "Proclamations, February 3, 1983," http://www.reagan.utexas.edu/archives/speeches/1983/20383b.htm (accessed January 26, 2015).

22. Nick Wing, "Atheists Lose Battle to Have 'In God We Trust' Removed From U.S. Currency," Huff Post Politics, September 12, 2013, http://www.huffingtonpost.com/2013/09/12/atheists-in-god-we-trust_n_3916762.html (accessed January 26, 2015).

23. Ibid.

24. Boycott the Pledge, http://www.dontsaythepledge.com/ (accessed January 26, 2015).

25. Pat Schatzline, *I Am Remnant* (Lake Mary, FL: Charisma House, 2014), 1.

26. Oswald Chambers, "You Are Not Your Own," http://utmost.org/you-are-not-your-own/ (accessed January 26, 2015).

Chapter 2
How Could God Use Me?

1. Adapted from *Men 4 God* (blog), "The Big List of Excuses Why God Can't Use You," February 16, 2008, http://menforgod .net/2008/02/16/the-big-list-of-excuses-why-god-cant-use-you/ (accessed January 27, 2015).

Chapter 3
The Messiah's Misfits

1. Dictionary.com, s.v. "misfit," http://dictionary.reference .com/browse/misfit (accessed January 27, 2015).

2. Urban Dictionary, s.v. "misfit," http://www.urbandictionary .com/define.php?term=Misfit (accessed January 27, 2015).

3. The Salvation Army, "William Booth," http://tinyurl .com/73bavt3 (accessed January 27, 2015).

Chapter 4
You Are Not Plan B

1. Doug Stanglin, "Judge OKs 'Morning-After Pill' for Girls of All Ages," *USA Today*, April 5, 2013, http://www.usatoday.com/ story/news/nation/2013/04/05/morning-after-pill-judge-plan-b -girls/2055873/ (accessed January 28, 2015).

2. *The 700 Club*, "Reinhard Bonnke: Setting Souls on Fire," http://www.cbn.com/700club/guests/bios/Reinhard_ Bonnke091306.aspx (accessed January 28, 2015).

3. Biblehub.com, s.v. "musterion," http://biblehub.com/ greek/3466.htm (accessed January 28, 2015).

4. Lee Shiu Hung, *Journal of the Royal Society of Medicine* 96, no. 8 (August 2003): 374–378, http://www.ncbi.nlm.nih.gov/pmc/ articles/PMC539564/ (accessed January 28, 2015).

5. Erik Eckholm, "China Suspends Adoptions and Sets Edict to Fight SARS," *New York Times*, May 16, 2003, http:// www.nytimes.com/2003/05/16/international/asia/16CHIN.html (accessed January 28, 2015).

Chapter 5
Royalty Sometimes Comes Broken

1. Chana Weisberg, "Nitzevet, Mother of David," http://www.chabad.org/theJewishWoman/article_cdo/aid/280331/jewish/Nitzevet-Mother-of-David.htm (accessed January 28, 2015).

2. Biblestudytools.com, s.v. "Mephibosheth," http://www.biblestudytools.com/dictionary/mephibosheth/ (accessed February 16, 2015).

3. Biblestudytools.com, s.v. "Lo-debar," http://www.biblestudytools.com/dictionary/lo-debar/ (accessed February 16, 2015).

4. Wikipedia.org, s.v. "Lo-debar," http://en.wikipedia.org/wiki/Lo-debar (accessed February 16, 2015).

Chapter 6
The Separation

1. Dictionary.com, s.v. "contagion," http://dictionary.reference.com/browse/contagion (accessed February 16, 2015).

2. Wikipedia.org, s.v. "yoke," http://en.wikipedia.org/wiki/Yoke (accessed February 16, 2015).

3. Studylight.org, s.v. "Belial," http://www.studylight.org/encyclopedias/tje/view.cgi?n=2805 (accessed February 16, 2015).

4. Edward Shorter, "Sad, Worthless, Hopeless?" Psychology Today, http://www.psychologytoday.com/blog/how-everyone-became-depressed/201406/sad-worthless-hopeless (accessed March 5, 2015).

5. Jennifer LeClaire, "Why Are so Many Pastors Committing Suicide?", Charisma News, December 11, 2013, http://www.charismanews.com/opinion/watchman-on-the-wall/42063-why-are-so-many-pastors-committing-suicide (accessed February 16, 2015).

6. Britannica.com, "Battle of Gettysburg," http://www.britannica.com/EBchecked/topic/232210/Battle-of-Gettysburg (accessed February 16, 2015).

Chapter 7
Rehiring the Holy Spirit

1. Biblehub.com, "Romans 1:28," http://biblehub.com/commentaries/gill/romans/1.htm (accessed February 16, 2015).

Chapter 8
Wilderness Wanderers

1. Schatzline, *I Am Remnant.*
2. John Bevere, *Victory in the Wilderness: Growing Strong in Dry Times* (Palmer Lake, CO: Messenger Press, 2002), 25–26.

Chapter 9
The Eight Insatiable Absolutes of the Unqualified

1. Goodreads.com, "Winston Churchill Quotes," http://www .goodreads.com/quotes/4970-when-the-eagles-are-silent-the -parrots-begin-to-jabber (accessed February 17, 2015).
2. Dictionary.com, s.v. "insatiable," http://dictionary.reference .com/browse/insatiable (accessed February 17, 2015).
3. Bibletools.com, s.v. "anegkletos," http://www.bibletools.org/ index.cfm/fuseaction/Lexicon.show/ID/G410/anegkletos.htm (accessed February 17, 2015).
4. Biblehub.com, s.v. "gebulah," http://biblehub.com/ hebrew/1367.htm (accessed February 17, 2015).
5. Gene Edwards, *A Tale of Three Kings* (Carol Stream, IL: Tyndale, 1992), 12.
6. C. S. Lewis, *The World's Last Night and Other Essays* (New York: Houghton Mifflin Harcourt, 2002), 9. Viewed at Google Books.

Chapter 10
You Can't Cut My Hair!

1. Leonard Ravenhill, "Weeping Between the Porch and the Altar," http://www.ravenhill.org/weeping2.htm (accessed February 17, 2015).
2. Lila Rose, "Five Things About Obama's Pro-Abortion Record Before You Vote," LifeNews.com, November 6, 2012, http://www.lifenews.com/2012/11/06/five-things-about-obamas -pro-abortion-record-before-you-vote/ (accessed February 17, 2015).
3. Biblehub.com, s.v. "shemen," http://biblehub.com/ hebrew/8081.htm (accessed February 17, 2015).
4. Biblestudytools.com, s.v. "chrio," http://www .biblestudytools.com/lexicons/greek/nas/chrio.html (accessed February 17, 2015).

Chapter 12
Get Your Feet Ready

1. The Last Days Calendar, "From Adam to Noah – Man's Wickedness, Nephilim and the Flood," http://lastdayscalendar .tripod.com/genesis_5___6.htm (accessed February 17, 2015).

Chapter 13
You Are God's Hashtag

1. William Booth, as quoted in Alvin Reid, *Evangelism Handbook: Spiritual, Intentional, Missional* (Nashville: B&H Publishing Group, 2009), 285. Viewed at Google Books.

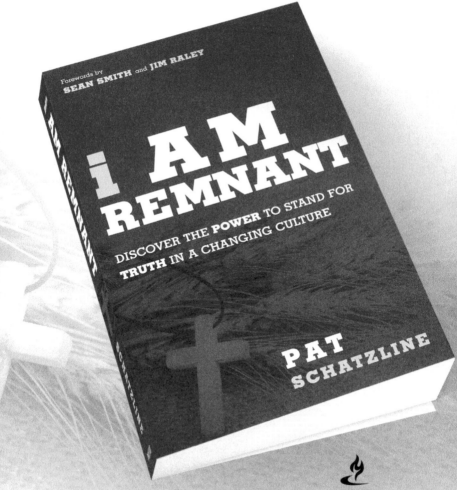

Don't Believe The Lies!

God is not angry with you, He loves you more than you know. In this book, Pat Schatzline introduces you to a God who accepts you, transforms you, and gives you a future filled with abundant blessing and opportunity.

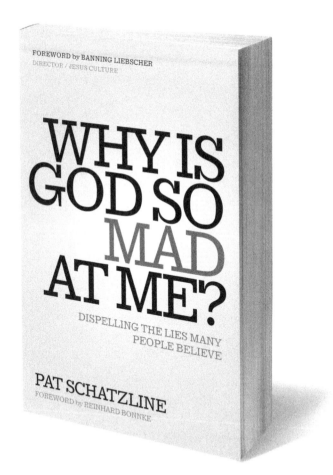

FOREWORD by BANNING LIEBSCHER
DIRECTOR / JESUS CULTURE

WHY IS GOD SO MAD AT ME?

DISPELLING THE LIES MANY PEOPLE BELIEVE

PAT SCHATZLINE
FOREWORD by REINHARD BONNKE